JERUSALEM TRAVEL GUIDE

2023

A Pilgrim's Companion to

the Holy City

HENRY PRICE

TABLE OF CONTENT

OPENING NOTE:

Seventeen years ago, during my time as a lecturer in the seminary, I embarked on my inaugural pilgrimage to Jerusalem. This experience had a profound impact on my life! I only regret not making the trip sooner, as it completely transformed the way I interpreted the Bible, particularly the accounts of Jesus and his disciples.

Through a single visit, the geographical settings described in the scriptures became tangible and real, within my grasp. I can still vividly recall the astonishing afternoon when I ascended the Mount of Olives, providing me with an incredible view of the magnificent Holy City, Jerusalem. The garden of Gethsemane, the Pool of

Bethesda, and Pilate's Judgment Hall were imprinted in my memory on that unforgettable day.

A few days later, the mesmerizing blue waters of the Sea of Galilee and the buoyant saltiness of the Dead Sea left an indelible mark on my consciousness. Each location, from Bethlehem to Manger Square and the Church of the Nativity, breathed new life into the biblical narratives, presenting them in a fresh and tangible way for me as a Bible student.

I ardently desire that every Christian could embark on this pilgrimage at least once. The beauty of a trip to Jerusalem lies in the fact that the stories from the Bible come alive, as you stand upon the very ground where sacred history unfolded. You visit the places where Jesus walked, lived, taught, performed miracles, where he was crucified, and where he triumphantly rose from the dead.

Dear pilgrim, I encourage you to study this travel guide in detail as you prepare to undertake your pilgrimage. The details herein this travel guide are very descriptive, giving you a clear picture of what lies in wait ahead of your journey.

INTRODUCTION TO JERUSALEM

Dear Pilgrim, you are about to submerge yourself to the enchanting city of Jerusalem with this comprehensive and carefully researched masterpiece. Jerusalem is a mesmerizing destination that has captivated the hearts and minds of travelers for centuries. Nestled in the heart of the Middle East, this ancient metropolis is a treasure trove of history, culture, and spirituality, making it one of the most compelling and sought-after pilgrimage sites in the world.

Jerusalem holds a unique place in the annals of human civilization, with a rich tapestry of narratives interwoven through its streets. With a history spanning over 3,000 years, it has been a center of political, religious, and cultural significance for countless civilizations, including the ancient Israelites, Romans, Byzantines, Arabs, Crusaders, Ottomans, and the modern State of Israel.

The city is revered by three major world religions - Judaism, Christianity, and Islam - each leaving an indelible mark on its landscapes. Jerusalem's Old City, a UNESCO World Heritage site, lies at the core of these spiritual traditions, and its ancient walls enclose an array of sacred sites that draw pilgrims and visitors from across the globe.

Exploring the Old City is a journey through time, as you stroll along its narrow, labyrinthine streets, breathing in the scents of incense and spices wafting from bustling markets. Enter through one of the seven gates and immerse yourself in the layers of history that unfold before your eyes. Here, you'll find the Western Wall, a holy site for Jews, where faithful visitors offer their prayers and wishes, and the Church of the Holy Sepulchre, believed to be the site of Jesus Christ's crucifixion and resurrection, a profound destination for Christians.

Beyond the spiritual realm, Jerusalem is a vibrant and cosmopolitan city that pulsates with life. Modern neighborhoods, such as West Jerusalem, offer a bustling cityscape filled with trendy cafes, upscale boutiques, and a thriving culinary scene. As you navigate the lively streets, you'll encounter a diverse tapestry of cultures, languages, and traditions, reflecting the city's melting pot of inhabitants and visitors from around the world.

But Jerusalem is not just a city frozen in time. It is a place where ancient history meets contemporary innovation. The vibrant art scene, with its numerous galleries and museums, showcases the city's creative spirit, while the emerging tech sector fuels an atmosphere of entrepreneurship and innovation.

Venture beyond the city limits, and you'll discover a landscape of breathtaking beauty. The surrounding hills, such as the Mount of Olives and Mount Zion, offer panoramic views of the city below, providing a serene retreat from the urban bustle. The nearby

Judean Desert beckons adventurers with its rugged terrain, ancient monasteries, and the awe-inspiring Masada fortress perched atop a cliff.

As you embark on your journey through Jerusalem, let this travel guide be your trusted companion. Whether you're a history enthusiast seeking ancient relics, a spiritual seeker yearning for enlightenment, or simply an intrepid traveler ready to explore new horizons, Jerusalem promises an unforgettable experience. Uncover its layers of heritage, connect with its diverse inhabitants, savor its culinary delights, and witness the unique harmony of the ancient and the contemporary that defines this remarkable city.

Jerusalem awaits you, ready to share its tales, secrets, and profound beauty. Get ready to embark on an extraordinary adventure that will leave an indelible imprint on your soul. This travel guide presents a clear picture of all that awaits you in Jerusalem.

CHAPTER ONE

BRIEF HISTORY AND SIGNIFICANCE OF JERUSALEM

The city of Jerusalem holds an incredibly rich and diverse history that spans over thousands of years. It is regarded as one of the oldest cities in the world, with evidence of human settlement dating back to the 4th millennium BCE. Jerusalem's historical and religious significance is unparalleled, as it serves as a holy site for the three major Abrahamic religions: Judaism, Christianity, and Islam. This convergence of religious importance has made Jerusalem a focal point of conflict and tension throughout history.

The early history of Jerusalem is closely tied to the biblical accounts found in the Hebrew Bible, known as the Old Testament in Christianity. According to these texts, Jerusalem was established as the capital city of the United Kingdom of Israel under King David in the 10th century BCE. His son, King Solomon, built the First Temple in Jerusalem, which became a central place of worship for the Israelites. However, Jerusalem faced multiple invasions and conquests over the centuries.

One of the most significant events in Jerusalem's history occurred in 586 BCE when the Babylonians, led by King Nebuchadnezzar, sacked the city and destroyed the First Temple. The Jewish people were subsequently exiled to Babylon.

After the Babylonian Empire fell, the Persian Empire took control of Jerusalem, and some Jews were allowed to return and rebuild the city and the Second Temple.

The city changed hands several times over the centuries. In 332 BCE, Alexander the Great conquered Jerusalem, followed by the Ptolemaic and Seleucid dynasties. Eventually, in 63 BCE, the Roman general Pompey conquered Jerusalem and incorporated it into the Roman Empire. This marked the beginning of Roman rule over the city.

During the 1st century CE, Jerusalem witnessed the life and crucifixion of Jesus Christ, which would have a profound impact on Christianity. After Jesus' death, the city became a significant center for early Christian communities. However, tensions between the Jewish population and the Roman authorities escalated, leading to a Jewish revolt in 66 CE. In response, the Romans, under the command of Titus, destroyed the Second Temple in 70 CE. This event, known as the Siege of Jerusalem, resulted in the dispersal of Jews throughout the Roman Empire, marking the beginning of the Jewish diaspora.

Jerusalem remained under Roman rule until the 4th century when Emperor Constantine converted to Christianity and issued the Edict of Milan, granting religious tolerance to Christians. In 326 CE, Constantine's mother, Helena, embarked on a pilgrimage to Jerusalem and initiated the construction of Christian holy sites, including the Church of the Holy Sepulchre, which is believed to be the site of Jesus' crucifixion and resurrection.

In the 7th century CE, the city came under Islamic rule when the Muslim armies, led by Caliph Umar, conquered Jerusalem in 638 CE. Islam recognized Jerusalem as a holy city and built the Al-Aqsa Mosque and the Dome of the Rock on the Temple Mount, which is considered the third holiest site in Islam. Jerusalem subsequently passed through the hands of various Muslim dynasties, including the Abbasids, Fatimids, Seljuks, and Ayyubids.

During the Crusades, which took place between the 11th and 13th centuries,

Jerusalem became a focal point of conflict between Christian crusaders from Europe and Muslim forces. The Crusaders captured Jerusalem in 1099 and established the Kingdom of Jerusalem, which lasted until 1187 when the Muslim leader Saladin recaptured the city.

In the following centuries, Jerusalem changed hands multiple times, with control shifting between the Mamluks, Ottomans, and various European powers during the colonial era. The city experienced periods of prosperity and decline, but its religious significance continued to draw pilgrims from around the world.

After the collapse of the Ottoman Empire at the end of World War I, Jerusalem came under the British Mandate for Palestine. However, tensions between Jewish and Arab communities grew, and the United Nations proposed a partition plan in 1947 to divide Palestine into separate Jewish and Arab states, with Jerusalem being placed under international administration due to its religious significance.

The 1948 Arab-Israeli War erupted soon after, leading to the establishment of the State of Israel and the division of Jerusalem. West Jerusalem came under Israeli control, while East Jerusalem, including the Old City and its holy sites, fell under Jordanian control. This division created a physical and political separation between Jewish and Arab communities and added a new layer of complexity to the conflict over Jerusalem.

The Six-Day War in 1967 marked a turning point in Jerusalem's history. Israel launched a preemptive strike against neighboring Arab countries, leading to the capture of East Jerusalem and the reunification of the city. Israel declared Jerusalem as its united and eternal capital, a move that has been widely disputed by the international community, which generally does not recognize Israel's sovereignty over East Jerusalem.

Since the reunification, Jerusalem has remained a contentious issue in Israeli-Palestinian relations and a major obstacle in peace negotiations. Both Israelis and Palestinians claim the city as their rightful capital, making it one of the core issues in the Israeli-Palestinian conflict.

In addition to the religious significance, Jerusalem is also home to numerous historical and archaeological sites, including the Western Wall, the Church of the Holy Sepulchre, the Al-Aqsa Mosque, and the Mount of Olives, to name just a few. These sites attract millions of visitors each year, further highlighting the city's cultural and historical importance.

The significance of Jerusalem extends far beyond its physical boundaries. It has become a symbol of religious devotion, national identity, and political struggle. Its complex history and diverse cultural heritage make it a unique and cherished city for people around the world. The future of Jerusalem remains a critical issue in achieving a lasting peace in the region and finding a resolution to the Israeli-Palestinian conflict.

OVERVIEW OF THE CITY'S CULTURAL, RELIGIOUS, AND POLITICAL IMPORTANCE:

Jerusalem holds immense cultural, religious, and political significance and is one of the most historically and emotionally charged cities in the world. Its importance stems from its rich history, as well as its significance to multiple religions and its complex political situation. Here's an overview of Jerusalem's cultural, religious, and political importance:

Cultural Importance:

Historical Heritage: Jerusalem has a history that spans over 3,000 years, with numerous archaeological sites and landmarks, including the Western Wall, the Church of the Holy Sepulchre, and the Dome of the Rock. These sites are not only religiously significant but also serve as cultural touchstones and symbols of the city's past.

Diversity: Jerusalem is a melting pot of cultures, with a diverse population comprising Jews, Muslims, Christians, and other religious and ethnic groups. The city's multiculturalism has contributed to its vibrant arts, music, cuisine, and traditions.

Museums and Cultural Institutions: Jerusalem is home to several world-renowned museums, such as the Israel Museum, which houses significant archaeological artifacts, Jewish art, and contemporary works. The city also hosts various cultural events, festivals, and exhibitions throughout the year.

Religious Importance:

Judaism: Jerusalem is considered the holiest city in Judaism. The Western Wall, the last remaining remnant of the ancient Jewish Temple, is a site of deep religious significance and a place of prayer and pilgrimage for Jews worldwide.

Christianity: Jerusalem is central to Christianity. The Church of the Holy Sepulchre, located in the Old City, is believed to be the site of Jesus' crucifixion, burial, and resurrection. Many Christian denominations have historical ties and religious institutions in the city.

Islam: Jerusalem is the third holiest city in Islam. The Dome of the Rock, situated on the Temple Mount, is a revered site where Muslims believe the Prophet Muhammad ascended to heaven. The Al-Aqsa Mosque, adjacent to the Dome, is also a significant place of worship.

Political Importance:

International Dispute: Jerusalem's political status has long been a subject of contention between Israel and Palestine. The city is claimed as the capital by both sides, and its final status is a crucial aspect of any peace negotiations between the parties involved.

Israeli Government: The Israeli government considers Jerusalem its capital and houses the country's political institutions there, including the Knesset (Parliament), the Prime Minister's Office, and various government ministries.

Palestinian Aspirations: The Palestinians envision East Jerusalem as the capital of their future state. The status of Jerusalem is a key point of contention in Israeli-Palestinian negotiations and has a significant impact on the broader Middle East peace process.

It's important to note that the situation in Jerusalem is complex and evolving. The perspectives and narratives regarding the city's cultural, religious, and political importance may vary depending on different sources and stakeholders involved.

GETTING TO JERUSALEM:

As a religious pilgrimage center, the City of Jerusalem attracts millions of visitors from around the world each year. Getting to Jerusalem is relatively easy due to its central location and well-connected transportation networks. There are various means of reaching this iconic destination, and each offers a unique experience. Let's explore the different ways you can travel to Jerusalem.

Air Travel:

The most convenient and time-saving option for international visitors is to fly directly to Jerusalem. The nearest major airport is Ben Gurion International Airport, located around 50 kilometers west of Jerusalem. It is one of the busiest airports in the Middle East and offers excellent connectivity to numerous destinations worldwide. From the airport, you can easily reach Jerusalem by taxi, private transfer, or public transportation.

Public Transportation:

a. Trains: Israel has a modern and efficient railway system. The train station at Ben Gurion Airport connects directly to Jerusalem. The journey takes around 25-30 minutes and offers a comfortable and scenic ride. There are also train services connecting Jerusalem to other major cities in Israel, such as Tel Aviv and Haifa.

b. Buses: Buses are a popular means of transportation within Israel, including Jerusalem. Egged, the national bus company, operates an extensive network of routes connecting Jerusalem to various cities and towns across the country. The Central Bus Station in Jerusalem serves as a major hub, and you can easily find buses to and from different locations.

Private Transportation:

a. Taxis: Taxis are widely available in Jerusalem and can be a convenient option, especially if you have a lot of luggage or prefer a door-to-door service. You can find taxis at the airport, major hotels, and designated taxi stands throughout the city. It is advisable to negotiate the fare or use the meter to ensure a fair price.

b. Rental Cars: Renting a car provides flexibility and independence, allowing you to explore not only Jerusalem but also the surrounding areas at your own pace. Many well-known car rental companies operate in Israel, and you can pick up a rental car at the airport or various locations within Jerusalem. However, keep in mind that driving in Jerusalem's Old City can be challenging due to narrow streets and limited parking options.

Pilgrimages and Religious Tours:

Jerusalem holds deep religious significance for Judaism, Christianity, and Islam. Many people visit Jerusalem as part of religious pilgrimages or organized tours. These tours often include transportation arrangements, making it easier for participants to reach

Jerusalem and explore its holy sites with the guidance of knowledgeable guides.

Walking and Cycling:

If you are in the vicinity of Jerusalem or prefer an adventurous approach, walking or cycling can be an excellent way to get to the city. The Israel National Trail, a long-distance hiking trail, passes near Jerusalem, allowing nature enthusiasts to embark on a memorable journey on foot. Additionally, there are cycling routes connecting Jerusalem to nearby regions, providing an alternative mode of transportation for the more active travelers.

As with any travel plans, it is essential to check the latest information, including travel advisories and transportation schedules, before your trip to Jerusalem. While the means of transportation may vary, reaching Jerusalem is relatively straightforward due to its significance as a global destination. Regardless of how you choose to get there, your journey to Jerusalem is sure to be filled with historical, cultural, and spiritual experiences that will leave a lasting impression.

TRANSPORTATION OPTIONS IN JERUSALEM:

Transportation options within Jerusalem provide convenient ways for residents and visitors to navigate the city and explore its numerous attractions. As the capital of Israel and one of the oldest cities in the world, Jerusalem offers various modes of transportation to accommodate different travel preferences and needs. From traditional methods to modern innovations, here is a comprehensive overview of the transportation options available within Jerusalem.

Public Buses: The public bus system in Jerusalem is extensive and serves as the primary mode of transportation for many residents. Egged, the largest bus company in Israel, operates numerous routes throughout the city, connecting different neighborhoods, tourist sites, and suburbs. The buses are affordable, reliable, and often run on a frequent schedule, including on Shabbat (Sabbath) and Jewish holidays.

Light Rail: Jerusalem's light rail system, known as the Jerusalem Light Rail, provides a convenient and efficient way to travel within the city. The light rail network currently consists of one line, which runs from the northern neighborhood of Pisgat Ze'ev through the city center to Mount Herzl in the southwest. The light rail operates from early morning until late at night, offering a comfortable and modern mode of transportation for both residents and tourists.

Taxis: Taxis are readily available throughout Jerusalem and are a popular choice for those seeking a more direct and personalized transportation experience. Licensed taxis can be hailed from designated taxi ranks, found at popular locations such as transportation hubs, hotels, and tourist sites. Alternatively, mobile ride-hailing apps like Uber and Gett also operate in Jerusalem, providing additional convenience and accessibility.

Sheruts: Sheruts, or shared taxis, are a unique and cost-effective transportation option within Jerusalem. These minivans typically follow fixed routes and can be flagged down along major streets or at specific stops. Sheruts usually have a set number of passengers, and fares are often lower than regular taxis. While they may take longer than private taxis due to multiple stops, they offer a shared experience and an opportunity to interact with locals.

Rental Cars: Renting a car provides flexibility and convenience, especially for travelers who want to explore Jerusalem and its surrounding areas at their own pace. Several car rental companies operate within the city, and there are various pick-up and drop-off locations available. However, it is essential to note that driving in Jerusalem can be challenging due to the narrow streets, heavy traffic, and complex road system.

Bicycles: Jerusalem offers an expanding network of cycling lanes and paths, promoting eco-friendly transportation options. The city has implemented a bike-sharing program called "Jerusalem Bikes," providing rental bicycles at numerous docking stations across the city. Tourists and residents can rent bikes for a short period or subscribe to long-term membership plans, making it an enjoyable and healthy way to explore the city.

Walking: Jerusalem's rich history, narrow alleys, and vibrant neighborhoods make it an ideal city for walking. Many of the major tourist attractions, including the Old City with its religious sites, are best explored on foot. Walking allows visitors to experience the city's unique atmosphere, discover hidden gems, and interact with locals. It is worth noting that some areas may involve uphill or uneven terrain, so comfortable footwear is recommended.

In addition to these transportation options, Jerusalem also benefits from accessibility features such as ramps, elevators, and designated parking spaces for individuals with disabilities. The city continues to invest in improving transportation infrastructure, enhancing public transportation services, and promoting sustainable mobility.

It's important to check current schedules, fares, and any specific regulations or restrictions before using any mode of transportation in Jerusalem. Information can be obtained from official tourism websites, transportation authorities, or local information centers.

Overall, Jerusalem provides a diverse range of transportation options, allowing residents and visitors to navigate the city efficiently, explore its unique attractions, and experience the rich cultural and historical heritage it offers.

BEST TIME TO VISIT:

With its rich tapestry of traditions and landmarks, choosing the best time to visit Jerusalem can greatly enhance your experience and ensure a memorable trip. Factors such as weather, crowds, and religious events play a significant role in determining the ideal time to explore this enchanting city.

One of the primary considerations when planning a trip to Jerusalem is the weather. The city experiences a Mediterranean climate, characterized by hot, dry summers and cool, wet winters. The summer months, from June to August, can be scorching, with temperatures frequently exceeding 30°C (86°F). The intense heat can make outdoor activities uncomfortable, and the tourist sites are often crowded during this period. If you can tolerate the heat, summer can be a suitable time to visit if you plan your activities early in the morning or late in the afternoon.

On the other hand, spring (March to May) and autumn (September to November) are generally considered the best seasons to visit Jerusalem. During these months, the weather is mild and pleasant, with average temperatures ranging from 15°C to 25°C (59°F to 77°F). The blooming flowers and lush greenery add to the city's charm, making it an excellent time for outdoor exploration. However, it's worth noting that spring coincides with the Jewish holiday of Passover and Easter, which can lead to larger crowds and higher accommodation prices.

Winter, from December to February, is the low season in Jerusalem. The temperatures can drop to around 10°C (50°F), and rainfall is more frequent. While the city might be quieter during this time, it offers a unique atmosphere, especially during the Christmas season. The Old City comes alive with colorful decorations, and Christian pilgrims gather to celebrate the birth of Jesus. It's important to pack warm clothing and an umbrella to navigate the occasional rain showers.

Another factor to consider when planning your visit to Jerusalem is religious events and holidays. Jerusalem is a spiritual center for Judaism, Christianity, and Islam, and the city is home to many significant religious sites. It's advisable to research and be aware of major events such as Easter, Passover, Hanukkah, and Ramadan, as these times can attract large numbers of pilgrims and tourists. While witnessing these religious celebrations can be a fascinating experience, it's essential to plan ahead and make any necessary reservations well in advance.

To avoid the peak tourist season, it's advisable to plan your visit to Jerusalem during the shoulder months, which are the periods just before or after the high season. These months include April, May, September, and October. During these times, the weather is pleasant, and the crowds are relatively smaller compared to the summer months. This allows for a more relaxed and immersive experience, whether you're exploring the ancient streets of the Old City, visiting the Western Wall, or walking along the Via Dolorosa.

In a nutshell, choosing the best time to visit Jerusalem depends on personal preferences and priorities. If you can tolerate the heat and larger crowds, summer might suit you. Spring and autumn offer comfortable weather and vibrant landscapes, while winter provides a unique atmosphere during the holiday season. Considering weather, crowds, and religious events, planning a trip to Jerusalem during the shoulder seasons like April, May, September, or October can strike a good balance between pleasant weather and manageable crowds. Regardless of the time you choose, a journey to Jerusalem promises to be a captivating experience filled with history, spirituality, and cultural treasures.

CHAPTER TWO: TOP ATTRACTIONS AND RELIGIOUS SITES

CHURCH OF THE HOLY SEPULCHER

The Church of the Holy Sepulchre, located in the heart of the Old City of Jerusalem, is one of the most significant and revered sites in Christianity. It stands on the spot believed to be the place where Jesus Christ was crucified, buried, and resurrected. This ancient and sacred pilgrimage site has a rich history spanning centuries, and its spiritual and historical importance attracts millions of visitors from around the world.

The origins of the Church of the Holy Sepulchre can be traced back to the fourth century when Constantine the Great, the

Roman Emperor, embraced Christianity and initiated the construction of churches in various holy sites. The emperor's mother, Saint Helena, embarked on a pilgrimage to Jerusalem and identified the location of Jesus' crucifixion and burial.

The church is built over a complex series of interconnected structures that include the Golgotha, or the Hill of Calvary, where Jesus was crucified, as well as the Holy Sepulchre, the burial site. It also encompasses other significant areas such as the Stone of Anointing, the Chapel of Adam, and the Chapel of the Finding of the True Cross.

Stepping inside the church, visitors are immediately struck by its grandeur and the aura of sanctity that pervades the space. The interior is a testament to the architectural styles and influences of different periods. The main entrance leads to the Stone of Anointing, a large stone slab where tradition holds that Jesus' body was prepared for burial. This spot is revered by pilgrims, who often touch or kiss the stone as an act of devotion.

The most sacred area of the church lies beyond the Stone of Anointing. The Edicule, an ornate structure, surrounds the Holy Sepulchre itself. The Holy Sepulchre is a small chamber that encloses the tomb where Jesus is said to have been laid to rest before his resurrection. Pilgrims can enter the Edicule and witness the empty tomb, which is an emotionally charged experience for many believers.

The Church of the Holy Sepulchre is also home to various Christian denominations, including the Greek Orthodox, Roman Catholic, Armenian Apostolic, Coptic Orthodox, and Ethiopian Orthodox churches. Each denomination maintains its own designated areas within the church, reflecting a delicate balance of coexistence and shared stewardship.

This coexistence, however, has not always been harmonious, as different religious groups have historically engaged in conflicts and disputes over control of the church. These tensions have led to the establishment of the "Status Quo," an agreement that governs the administration and division of the church among the different denominations. Under this arrangement, the smallest changes, such as the relocation of a chair or the rearrangement of a candlestick, require the consensus of all parties involved.

Despite the challenges, the Church of the Holy Sepulchre remains a symbol of unity and faith for Christians worldwide. It serves as a destination for pilgrims who seek to deepen their spiritual connection to the life and teachings of Jesus Christ. Countless individuals embark on arduous journeys, often spanning continents, to reach this sacred site and participate in the rich liturgical traditions and rituals that take place within its walls.

Beyond its spiritual significance, the Church of the Holy Sepulchre is also a cultural and historical treasure. Its architectural beauty, adorned with intricate mosaics, vibrant frescoes, and ornate decorations, reflects the artistic styles of different eras. The church stands as a living testament to the enduring legacy of Christianity and the enduring impact of the events that unfolded in Jerusalem over two thousand years ago.

In conclusion, the Church of the Holy Sepulchre stands as an enduring symbol of faith, history, and devotion. It is a place of deep spiritual significance, where believers from around the world come to connect with the life and teachings of Jesus Christ. As a testament to its importance, this ancient and sacred site continues to captivate and inspire countless individuals, leaving an indelible mark on their spiritual journeys.

ARMENIAN QUARTER AND ST JAMES CATHEDRAL

The Armenian Quarter in Jerusalem is a historic and culturally significant area located within the walls of the Old City of Jerusalem. It is one of the four quarters that make up the Old City, along with the Jewish, Christian, and Muslim Quarters. The Armenian Quarter holds immense historical and religious significance for the Armenian community worldwide.

The Armenian presence in Jerusalem dates back to the early Christian era, making it one of the oldest communities in the city. The Armenians trace their roots to the time of Jesus Christ and have maintained a continuous presence in Jerusalem for centuries. The community has faced numerous challenges throughout history, including persecution, wars, and political upheavals. However, they have managed to preserve their heritage and traditions in the Armenian Quarter.

The Armenian Quarter is home to several significant landmarks, but the most prominent and revered among them is the St. James Cathedral, also known as the Armenian Apostolic Church of St. James. This stunning cathedral stands as the spiritual center and heart of the Armenian community in Jerusalem. It is one of the most ancient Christian churches in the world and a vital pilgrimage site for Armenian Christians.

St. James Cathedral was originally built in the 4th century AD, though it has undergone several reconstructions and renovations over the centuries. The cathedral stands on the site where James the Apostle, also known as St. James the Greater, is believed to be buried. It is revered as his final resting place and attracts pilgrims from around the world.

The cathedral's architecture is a fascinating blend of different styles due to the various construction phases it has undergone. The exterior features a combination of Byzantine, Romanesque, and Gothic elements, while the interior showcases rich Armenian ecclesiastical art and design. The cathedral's stunning facade, intricate carvings, and beautiful frescoes make it a visually captivating structure.

Inside the St. James Cathedral, visitors can explore the intricately decorated chapels, the Holy Altar, and the tomb of St. James. The cathedral also houses a vast collection of religious artifacts, manuscripts, and religious relics, many of which have immense historical and cultural value. These treasures provide insights into the rich spiritual heritage and cultural contributions of the Armenian community.

The Armenian Quarter surrounding the St. James Cathedral is a maze of narrow streets, alleys, and courtyards. It is a vibrant and bustling neighborhood with residential buildings, shops, restaurants, and guesthouses. Walking through the quarter, one can experience the unique Armenian culture, taste traditional Armenian cuisine, and explore local crafts and souvenirs.

The Armenian presence in the quarter extends beyond the religious and cultural spheres. The community has also played an active role in education and philanthropy. The Armenian Patriarchate's Theological Seminary, located within the Armenian Quarter, is an esteemed educational institution that has produced generations of Armenian clergy, scholars, and intellectuals.

Despite the challenges faced over the centuries, the Armenian Quarter and St. James Cathedral stand as enduring symbols of the Armenian community's resilience and determination to preserve its heritage. The quarter serves as a testament to the rich tapestry of cultures and faiths that coexist within the walls of the Old City of Jerusalem.

Visiting the Armenian Quarter and St. James Cathedral offers a unique opportunity to delve into the rich history, spirituality, and cultural traditions of the Armenian people. It is a place where the ancient and the modern intertwine, providing visitors with a profound sense of connection to the past and a deeper understanding of the diverse religious and cultural fabric of Jerusalem.

TEMPLE MOUNT AND THE DOME OF THE ROCK

Temple Mount and the Dome of the Rock in Jerusalem are two iconic and historically significant structures that hold immense religious, cultural, and political significance. Situated in the heart of the Old City of Jerusalem, these landmarks have played a central role in shaping the city's history and remain sources of deep reverence and contention to this day.

Temple Mount, known as "Haram al-Sharif" in Arabic and "Har HaBayit" in Hebrew, is a rectangular esplanade encompassing approximately 35 acres. It is considered one of the most sacred sites in Judaism, Christianity, and Islam. The site has a long and complex history dating back thousands of years. According to Jewish tradition, it is believed to be the location of the First and Second Temples, which were the holiest sites in ancient Judaism. The First Temple was constructed by King Solomon in the 10th century BCE, while the Second Temple was rebuilt by King Herod in the 1st century BCE.

The destruction of the Second Temple by the Romans in 70 CE marked a significant turning point in Jewish history and led to the diaspora of the Jewish people. Since then, Temple Mount has been a focal point of Jewish longing and has remained a symbol of Jewish identity and national aspirations. Today, the Western Wall, a remnant of the Second Temple, stands at the southwestern corner of the Temple Mount and is considered the holiest site in Judaism.

The Dome of the Rock, an architectural marvel, stands at the center of Temple Mount. Built in the late 7th century CE, it is an Islamic shrine and a masterpiece of early Islamic architecture. The Dome of the Rock is revered by Muslims worldwide as the third holiest site in Islam, after Mecca and Medina. Its golden dome, intricate mosaics, and stunning geometric designs make it a significant symbol of Jerusalem's skyline.

The Dome of the Rock holds immense religious significance in Islam. It is believed to be the spot where the Prophet Muhammad ascended to heaven during the

Night Journey. The interior of the shrine features inscriptions from the Quran, showcasing the Islamic faith's central tenets. The exterior is adorned with vibrant blue tiles and intricate Arabic calligraphy, adding to its aesthetic beauty.

The coexistence of these two religiously significant structures on Temple Mount has made it a site of immense tension and conflict throughout history. The control and ownership of the area have been subject to rivalries between different religious and political groups. The complexities surrounding Temple Mount are tied to the broader Israeli-Palestinian conflict and have been a significant point of contention between Israelis and Palestinians.

The status quo arrangement, established after the Six-Day War in 1967, grants administrative control of the Temple Mount to the Islamic Waqf, a religious trust appointed by Jordan. Jewish prayer is allowed at the Western Wall, but non-Muslims are not permitted to pray on the Temple Mount itself, due to concerns about potential religious clashes. The delicate balance of managing the site has led to periodic outbreaks of violence and political disputes.

In recent years, tensions around Temple Mount and the Dome of the Rock have remained high, with sporadic clashes and protests. The political nature of the conflict has led to international scrutiny and attempts at mediation to find a lasting resolution. However, finding a mutually acceptable solution that respects the religious sensitivities and national aspirations of all parties involved remains an ongoing challenge.

Despite the challenges and complexities surrounding Temple Mount and the Dome of the Rock, their historical and cultural significance cannot be overstated. They serve as reminders of the deep religious devotion, historical heritage, and profound emotions that Jerusalem evokes in people of different faiths. As a result, these landmarks continue to shape the collective identity and aspirations of those who hold them dear and remain at the heart of the larger narrative of the Israeli-Palestinian conflict.

VIA DOLOROSA

The Via Dolorosa, also known as the Way of Sorrows or the Way of the Cross, is a significant pilgrimage route in Jerusalem, Israel. It is believed to be the path that Jesus Christ walked on his way to crucifixion. The Via Dolorosa holds immense religious and historical importance for Christians worldwide, as it symbolizes the final journey of Jesus leading up to his death and resurrection.

The route of the Via Dolorosa begins at the Antonia Fortress, where Jesus was tried and condemned by Pontius Pilate, and concludes at the Church of the Holy Sepulchre, which is believed to be the site of his crucifixion, burial, and resurrection. The path itself is approximately 600 meters (2,000 feet) long, winding through the narrow streets of the Old City of Jerusalem.

The Via Dolorosa consists of fourteen stations, each representing a specific event or moment during Jesus' Passion. These stations are marked along the route, allowing pilgrims to pause, reflect, and commemorate the corresponding event. The stations vary in significance, ranging from Jesus being condemned to death, carrying the cross, meeting his mother, falling multiple times, being crucified, and finally, being laid in the tomb.

As visitors walk along the Via Dolorosa, they experience the palpable sense of history and spirituality that permeates the narrow streets. The route is bustling with locals, tourists, and pilgrims from various Christian denominations, all united in their desire to retrace Jesus' footsteps and reflect on his sacrifice. The atmosphere is filled with prayers, hymns, and contemplation, creating a deeply profound and moving experience for those who undertake the journey.

While the Via Dolorosa is a significant spiritual site, it is also a reflection of the diverse cultural and religious heritage present in Jerusalem. The path traverses through different quarters of the Old City, including the Muslim Quarter, the Christian Quarter, and the Armenian Quarter. As pilgrims walk, they encounter bustling markets, ancient architecture, and sacred sites belonging to multiple faiths, creating a unique blend of cultures and traditions.

One of the most iconic and visited stations along the Via Dolorosa is the Church of the Holy Sepulchre. This church is believed to be built upon the site where Jesus was crucified, buried, and resurrected. Within its walls, pilgrims can visit the Calvary (Golgotha), where Jesus was crucified, and the Aedicule, a small shrine enclosing the tomb where Jesus was laid to rest. The Church of the Holy Sepulchre serves as the culmination of the Via Dolorosa pilgrimage, where pilgrims can offer their prayers, seek solace, and connect with their faith on a profound level.

The Via Dolorosa holds deep significance not only for religious pilgrims but also for historians and scholars interested in the life and times of Jesus Christ. It serves as a living testament to the events that unfolded over two thousand years ago and provides a tangible link to the past. The route has undergone numerous changes throughout history, reflecting the political, social, and religious dynamics of Jerusalem. The current path was established during the medieval period and has since been embraced by countless generations of believers.

In conclusion, the Via Dolorosa in Jerusalem stands as a timeless symbol of faith, sacrifice, and redemption. It is a sacred pilgrimage site that invites people from all walks of life to engage with the story of Jesus' final journey. By retracing the path he took, pilgrims can connect with their spirituality, deepen their understanding of the Christian faith, and experience the power of Jerusalem's rich religious and cultural heritage. The Via Dolorosa serves as a bridge between the past and the present, reminding us of the enduring legacy of Jesus' life, death, and resurrection.

HURVA SYNAGOGUE

The Hurva Synagogue, located in the heart of the Jewish Quarter of the Old City of Jerusalem, is a historically significant and architecturally remarkable synagogue. Its story spans centuries, characterized by destruction, restoration, and a symbol of resilience for the Jewish community.

The origins of the Hurva Synagogue can be traced back to the early 18th century. The synagogue was initially built by disciples of Rabbi Judah he-Hasid, who was a prominent Jewish leader at the time. The word "Hurva" means "ruin" in Hebrew, referring to the destroyed state of the previous synagogue in that location. The new synagogue became a central institution for the Jewish community in Jerusalem.

The original structure of the Hurva Synagogue featured a majestic dome, towering arches, and intricate decorations, showcasing a blend of Sephardic and Ashkenazi architectural styles. It became a symbol of Jewish religious and cultural identity in Jerusalem, serving as a place of worship, study, and community gathering.

However, in 1721, just a few years after its completion, the Hurva Synagogue was tragically destroyed in a violent attack led by local Muslim forces. The synagogue was left in ruins, and its desolation became a poignant reminder of the precariousness of Jewish life in Jerusalem.

For the next 140 years, the site of the Hurva Synagogue remained a ruin, with only the remnants of the building serving as a silent testament to its former glory. The Jewish community in Jerusalem dreamt of rebuilding their cherished synagogue, but political and financial challenges delayed their aspirations.

It was not until the late 19th century that plans for the reconstruction of the Hurva Synagogue began to take shape. With the support of Baron Edmond de Rothschild, a prominent philanthropist, the Jewish community was finally able to initiate the restoration process. The new synagogue, completed in 1864, reflected the architectural style of the time, incorporating elements of the Ottoman and European influences. The restoration of the Hurva Synagogue reinvigorated the Jewish community and re-established their presence in Jerusalem's Old City.

However, the renewed era of the Hurva Synagogue was short-lived. During the 1948 Arab-Israeli War, the synagogue once again fell victim to destruction. As Jordanian forces took control of the Jewish Quarter, they deliberately blew up the Hurva Synagogue, leaving only ruins behind.

For the next six decades, the ruins of the Hurva Synagogue served as a reminder of the painful past and the ongoing struggle for Jewish rights and sovereignty in Jerusalem. However, the dream of rebuilding the synagogue remained alive.

In 2000, plans for the reconstruction of the Hurva Synagogue were initiated once again. The project aimed not only to restore the synagogue but also to recreate its original grandeur and significance. Architects and historians meticulously studied the original plans, historical records, and photographs to ensure the accurate reproduction of the synagogue's distinct features.

After years of meticulous planning and construction, the restored Hurva Synagogue was inaugurated in March 2010. The new structure closely resembles the original, with its impressive dome, arched windows, and ornate decorations. The synagogue now stands as a symbol of the Jewish people's unwavering determination, resilience, and connection to their spiritual and cultural heritage.

Today, the Hurva Synagogue serves as a vibrant center for prayer, Torah study, and community activities. It has become one of the iconic landmarks in the Jewish Quarter of Jerusalem's Old City, attracting visitors from around the world who come to admire its beauty and learn about its rich history.

The story of the Hurva Synagogue is a testament to the enduring spirit of the Jewish people and their unwavering commitment to preserving their religious and cultural heritage. It stands as a symbol of resilience, hope, and the unbreakable bond between the Jewish people and Jerusalem, their eternal capital.

DORMITION ABBEY

Dormition Abbey, also known as the Abbey of the Dormition, is a prominent Christian religious complex located in Jerusalem,

Israel. Situated on Mount Zion, near the walls of the Old City, the abbey holds significant historical and religious importance for Christians around the world. It stands as a symbol of the Virgin Mary's passing from earthly life to heavenly rest, an event known as the Dormition of the Assumption.

The construction of Dormition Abbey began in 1900, commissioned by the German Benedictine Order. The design was inspired by Romanesque and Byzantine architectural styles, reflecting the rich Christian heritage of Jerusalem. The architects Heinrich Renard and Heinrich von Mauderlitz envisioned a grand structure that would serve as a place of worship and pilgrimage.

The abbey is adorned with intricate stone carvings, beautiful mosaics, and striking stained glass windows. Its imposing bell tower can be seen from afar, adding to the Jerusalem skyline. The interior of the abbey is equally impressive, featuring a high-vaulted nave, stunning murals depicting biblical scenes, and a serene atmosphere that invites reflection and prayer.

The focal point of Dormition Abbey is the Church of the Dormition, which occupies the central space of the complex. The church is dedicated to the Virgin Mary and commemorates her assumption into heaven. According to Christian tradition, the Virgin Mary fell into a peaceful sleep, and her body was then taken up to heaven by God. The church serves as a place of pilgrimage for many Christians who come to honor the memory of the Virgin Mary and seek spiritual solace.

Within the church, visitors can find the main altar, which is adorned with a magnificent mosaic depicting the Dormition of the Virgin Mary. The mosaic beautifully captures the moment of her passing, surrounded by the apostles, angels, and other biblical figures. The crypt beneath the main altar is believed to be the resting place of the Virgin Mary.

Aside from the Church of the Dormition, Dormition Abbey also encompasses a monastery, a guesthouse, and a peaceful garden. The monastery is home to the

Benedictine community, a group of monks dedicated to a life of prayer, study, and service. The guesthouse provides accommodations for pilgrims and visitors from around the world, offering a place of rest and spiritual retreat.

The abbey's garden, known as the "Hortus Conclusus" or Enclosed Garden, is a tranquil oasis amidst the bustling city of Jerusalem. With its lush greenery, aromatic flowers, and shaded seating areas, the garden offers a peaceful sanctuary for contemplation and meditation. It is a popular spot for visitors to find respite from their journey and connect with their spirituality.

Dormition Abbey has witnessed significant historical events and has weathered periods of turmoil and conflict. During World War I, the Ottoman Empire seized the abbey and expelled the monks. However, after the war, the German community regained control and restored the abbey to its former glory.

In more recent years, Dormition Abbey continues to be a place of religious significance and a beacon of interfaith dialogue. It serves as a meeting point for Christians from various denominations, as well as a place for dialogue with other religious communities in Jerusalem. The abbey also hosts regular liturgical services, including Masses, prayer vigils, and choral performances, which attract both locals and tourists seeking spiritual enrichment.

Conclusively, Dormition Abbey stands as a testament to the rich Christian heritage and the enduring legacy of the Virgin Mary in Jerusalem. Its stunning architecture, sacred artwork, and serene ambiance make it a must-visit destination for pilgrims and tourists alike. The abbey's significance goes beyond its religious associations, as it serves as a symbol of unity, peace, and dialogue among different faiths in this ancient city.

WESTERN WALL (WAILING WALL)

The Western Wall, also known as the Wailing Wall, holds great significance and is one of the most revered religious sites in the world. Located in the Old City of Jerusalem, this ancient structure serves as a testament to the rich history and spiritual significance of the region.

The Western Wall is a remnant of the Second Temple, which was destroyed by the Romans in 70 CE during the Jewish revolt. It is the only visible part of the Temple Mount that remains standing today. For centuries, it has served as a symbol of Jewish faith, resilience, and connection to the land of Israel.

The wall itself is made of massive limestone blocks, with some measuring over 40 feet in length. Its immense size and the craftsmanship involved in its construction are awe-inspiring. The wall is approximately 62 feet high, but only a small portion of it is visible above ground level. The rest of the wall extends deep into the earth, reaching beneath the modern city.

For Jews, the Western Wall is the holiest place of prayer. It is believed to be the closest spot to the Holy of Holies, the inner sanctuary of the Temple where the presence of God resided. Jews from around the world come to the Western Wall to offer prayers, recite Psalms, and place small notes with written prayers into its crevices. This practice has given the wall its alternative name, the "Wailing Wall," as many visitors express their sorrows, hopes, and aspirations through heartfelt prayers.

The Western Wall also holds deep historical and emotional significance for the Jewish people. It has witnessed the many trials and tribulations of the Jewish nation throughout history. From the destruction of the Temple to the exile and subsequent return, the Western Wall has remained a constant symbol of Jewish identity and resilience.

Over the centuries, various empires and ruling powers have controlled Jerusalem, and the Western Wall has experienced periods of neglect and desecration. However, with the establishment of the State of Israel in 1948 and the subsequent reunification of Jerusalem in 1967, the Western Wall returned to Jewish control. It has since become a vibrant center of Jewish religious life and an iconic symbol of the Jewish connection to the land.

Visiting the Western Wall is a deeply moving experience. As one approaches the wall, the atmosphere is charged with spiritual energy and devotion. Men and women have separate sections, and visitors are encouraged to dress modestly and observe the customs and traditions of the holy site. It is customary to approach the wall with reverence, touching the ancient stones and offering personal prayers.

The Western Wall Plaza, adjacent to the wall, is a bustling gathering place for worshippers, tourists, and locals alike. It is a site of celebration and reflection, hosting bar mitzvah ceremonies, weddings, and national events. The plaza also serves as a gateway to the various quarters of the Old City, offering a glimpse into the rich tapestry of cultures, religions, and traditions that coexist within its walls.

While the Western Wall is of utmost importance to the Jewish faith, it also holds significance for Christians and Muslims. For Christians, the wall represents a link to Jesus Christ, who walked and taught in Jerusalem. Many Christian pilgrims visit the wall as part of their spiritual journey. Muslims, too, revere the site as the location of the Al-Buraq Wall, associated with the Prophet Muhammad's mystical night journey.

The Western Wall stands as a symbol of unity and reverence for people of different faiths. It represents the intertwining history, spirituality, and cultural heritage that make

Jerusalem a city of profound significance to billions of people worldwide.

In conclusion, the Western Wall, or Wailing Wall, is a sacred site of immense historical, religious, and emotional importance. It serves as a powerful symbol of Jewish faith and resilience, as well as a unifying place of worship for people of various religious backgrounds. Visiting the Western Wall is a transformative experience that allows individuals to connect with the ancient past and find solace, hope, and inspiration. Its presence in Jerusalem continues to inspire awe and reverence, reminding us of the enduring power of faith and the significance of preserving historical heritage for future generations.

TOWER OF DAVID AND THE CITADEL

The Tower of David and the Citadel in Jerusalem are two iconic structures that hold great historical and cultural significance. Situated near the Jaffa Gate, one of the main entrances to the Old City of Jerusalem, they have witnessed countless chapters of the city's rich and tumultuous past. The Tower of David, also known as the Jerusalem Citadel, stands as a symbol of power, resilience, and the diverse layers of history that have shaped Jerusalem over the centuries.

The origins of the Tower of David can be traced back to the 2nd century BCE, during the Hasmonean period. However, the structure as we see it today is primarily a result of the renovations and additions made during the reign of King Herod in the 1st century BCE. King Herod, known for his ambitious architectural projects, fortified the city and constructed several structures, including the magnificent citadel.

Over the centuries, the Tower of David and the Citadel were repeatedly destroyed, rebuilt, and modified by different rulers and conquerors who sought to exert control over Jerusalem. It has served as a military fortress, a royal palace, a prison, and a garrison for various armies. Its strategic location offered commanding views of the city, making it an ideal site for defense.

One of the defining moments in the history of the Tower of David and the Citadel was the Roman siege of Jerusalem in 70 CE. The citadel withstood the Roman assault for several weeks until it finally fell, marking the end of Jewish sovereignty in Jerusalem. The Romans destroyed much of the city, including the Second Temple, leaving only the Western Wall standing.

During the Byzantine and Islamic periods, the Tower of David underwent significant changes. The Byzantines reinforced the citadel's defenses, while the Muslims transformed it into a residential palace and a symbol of Islamic rule. It was during this time that the citadel acquired the name "Tower of David," as a reference to the biblical King David, who was believed to have resided there.

In the medieval era, the Crusaders made their mark on the Tower of David. They added fortifications, expanded the complex, and used it as a stronghold. After the Crusader period, the citadel fell under the rule of various Islamic dynasties, including the Ayyubids and the Mamluks, who continued to modify and adapt the structure to their needs.

The Ottoman Empire gained control of Jerusalem in the 16th century and made further alterations to the Tower of David. They built a minaret and a clock tower, reflecting the architectural style of the time. During this period, the citadel served as an administrative center and a garrison for Ottoman troops.

In the 19th and early 20th centuries, as Jerusalem became a focus of international interest, the Tower of David underwent significant restoration efforts. British archaeologists and architects worked to preserve the historical integrity of the structure while adapting it to serve as a museum. The Tower of David Museum was officially opened in 1989 and offers visitors a captivating journey through the history of Jerusalem, utilizing multimedia exhibits, archaeological artifacts, and immersive displays.

Today, the Tower of David and the Citadel are an integral part of Jerusalem's skyline and serve as a prominent tourist attraction. The complex houses archaeological discoveries, exhibition spaces, and breathtaking views of the Old City and its surroundings. It also hosts cultural events, concerts, and light shows that enhance the visitor experience and bring the history of Jerusalem to life.

The Tower of David and the Citadel are not only architectural marvels but also bear witness to the diverse cultures, faiths, and historical events that have shaped Jerusalem throughout the centuries. They serve as a reminder of the city's resilience and the enduring significance of Jerusalem as a center of religious, cultural, and political importance.

MOUNT OF OLIVES AND THE GARDEN OF GETHSEMANE

The Mount of Olives and the Garden of Gethsemane in Jerusalem hold immense historical, religious, and cultural significance. Situated on the eastern side of the city, these two sites have witnessed numerous significant events throughout history and continue to attract pilgrims and tourists from around the world. Let us explore the rich history and importance of the Mount of Olives and the Garden of Gethsemane.

The Mount of Olives, also known as Mount Olivet, is a mountain ridge located to the east of Jerusalem's Old City. Rising to an elevation of around 800 meters, it offers breathtaking views of the city and its surroundings. The mountain is named after the olive groves that once covered its slopes, a symbol of peace, abundance, and spirituality in the region. It has served as a significant landmark throughout Jerusalem's history and has been mentioned in various religious texts, including the Bible and the Quran.

The Mount of Olives has particular significance in Christianity, Judaism, and Islam. In Christianity, it is closely associated with several key events in the life of Jesus Christ. According to the New Testament, Jesus often visited the Mount of Olives during his time in Jerusalem. It was from this mount that Jesus delivered the famous Sermon on the Mount, which contains some of his most profound teachings. The mountain is also linked to Jesus' Ascension, where he is believed to have ascended to heaven after his resurrection.

One of the most notable sites on the Mount of Olives is the Garden of Gethsemane, a tranquil and revered place located at the foot of the mountain. The word "Gethsemane" means "olive press" in Hebrew, indicating the presence of olive trees in the area. The garden holds immense significance for Christians as the place where Jesus prayed on the night before his crucifixion. It is here that Jesus experienced profound anguish and submitted to God's will, leading to his ultimate sacrifice for humanity's redemption.

The Garden of Gethsemane is known for its ancient olive trees, some of which are believed to be over 2,000 years old, potentially dating back to the time of Jesus. These gnarled and majestic trees add to the spiritual ambiance of the garden and serve as a powerful symbol of endurance and resilience.

Over the centuries, the Mount of Olives and the Garden of Gethsemane have been revered pilgrimage destinations for Christians. Many churches and religious institutions have been built in the area to commemorate the events associated with Jesus' life and ministry. One of the most prominent is the Church of All Nations, also known as the Basilica of the Agony, built near the Garden of Gethsemane. This beautiful church features stunning architecture and magnificent mosaics, and it houses the Rock of Agony, a rock said to be the very spot where Jesus prayed before his arrest.

Apart from its religious significance, the Mount of Olives holds historical and archaeological importance. It contains several ancient Jewish tombs, including the Tombs of the Prophets, which are believed to be the final resting places of biblical figures such as Zechariah and Haggai. The mountain also served as a route for processions during ancient Jewish festivals and is mentioned in Jewish texts as a place where the Messiah will appear in the future.

In addition to its religious and historical aspects, the Mount of Olives offers visitors breathtaking panoramic views of Jerusalem. The stunning vista from the mount allows one to appreciate the city's unique topography, including the Old City's iconic landmarks such as the Dome of the Rock, the Western Wall, and the Church of the Holy Sepulchre.

In conclusion, the Mount of Olives and the Garden of Gethsemane are two significant sites in Jerusalem that hold deep religious, historical, and cultural importance. They are closely associated with the life and teachings of Jesus Christ and serve as reminders of his sacrifice and the events leading to his crucifixion. These sacred places continue to inspire and attract pilgrims and visitors from all corners of the globe, offering a glimpse into the profound spiritual heritage of the region and providing a peaceful sanctuary for reflection and prayer.

YAD VASHEM HOLOCAUST MEMORIAL AND MUSEUM

Yad Vashem, located in Jerusalem, Israel, is one of the most significant Holocaust memorials and museums in the world. Established in 1953, Yad Vashem's primary mission is to commemorate the six million Jewish victims of the Holocaust and ensure that their memory lives on for future generations. The name "Yad Vashem" is derived from a biblical verse in Isaiah 56:5, meaning "a monument and a name" symbolizing the aim of preserving the names and memories of Holocaust victims.

Yad Vashem serves as a multifaceted institution encompassing various elements, including a museum, archives, research center, educational programs, and commemorative spaces. It offers a comprehensive exploration of the Holocaust, its causes, consequences, and human stories, while also emphasizing the importance of remembrance, education, and combating anti-Semitism.

The heart of Yad Vashem is its museum, a deeply moving and thought-provoking journey through the Holocaust experience. The museum is designed in a unique way, guiding visitors through a chronological narrative, from pre-war Jewish life to the systematic persecution and mass murder of Jews during World War II. The exhibition incorporates personal testimonies, artifacts, photographs, documents, and immersive audiovisual displays, creating a powerful and emotional experience that brings history to life. It aims to convey the individual human stories within the broader historical context, illustrating the tragedy and resilience of the Jewish people during those dark times.

Within the museum, the Hall of Names stands as a powerful tribute to the victims of the Holocaust. It is a circular space containing the largest database of Jewish Holocaust victims, currently holding millions of names collected from around the world. The names are inscribed on individual pages, symbolizing the importance of preserving the memory of each individual life lost.

Aside from the museum, Yad Vashem houses various other significant areas. The Children's Memorial, a poignant underground chamber, pays homage to the approximately 1.5 million Jewish children who perished in the Holocaust. It uses mirrors and atmospheric effects to create the illusion of an endless space, while continuously reciting the names, ages, and countries of origin of the children. The Avenue of the Righteous Among the Nations honors non-Jews who risked their lives to save Jews during the Holocaust, recognizing their courage and humanity.

Yad Vashem also plays a crucial role in research and education. Its archives and research center contain an extensive collection of historical records, testimonies, and artifacts, making it a significant resource for scholars and researchers worldwide. The institution conducts ongoing research and documentation projects, collecting survivor testimonies and gathering evidence to combat Holocaust denial and distortion.

Education is a central pillar of Yad Vashem's work. The International School for Holocaust Studies provides educational programs, seminars, and workshops for teachers, students, and educators from around the globe. These initiatives aim to foster an understanding of the Holocaust's historical significance and its broader ethical implications, encouraging critical thinking and reflection on issues of human rights, tolerance, and social responsibility.

Yad Vashem's impact extends beyond its physical location in Jerusalem. It collaborates with international institutions, museums, and organizations to raise awareness about the Holocaust and promote Holocaust education and remembrance worldwide. It also organizes exhibitions, traveling displays, and educational initiatives in different countries, ensuring that the lessons of the Holocaust reach diverse audiences.

In summary, Yad Vashem stands as a profound and essential institution dedicated to preserving the memory of the Holocaust and its victims. Through its museum, archives, educational programs, and commemorative spaces, it provides a platform for remembrance, research, education, and dialogue. By confronting the horrors of the past, Yad Vashem inspires individuals and societies to confront hatred, prejudice, and discrimination in the present and future, working towards a world where such atrocities are never repeated.

ISRAEL MUSEUM AND THE DEAD SEA SCROLLS

The Israel Museum and the Dead Sea Scrolls in Jerusalem are two intertwined facets of history, culture, and archaeological significance that offer a profound understanding of the past. The Israel Museum, located in Jerusalem, is the largest cultural institution in Israel and is renowned worldwide for its vast collection of art, archaeology, and Judaica. Within its sprawling complex, one of the most treasured and captivating exhibits is undoubtedly the Dead Sea Scrolls, a collection of ancient Jewish manuscripts discovered in the mid-20th century.

The Israel Museum itself is a testament to the rich tapestry of human creativity and heritage. It was established in 1965 and showcases over 500,000 objects spanning a vast range of periods and civilizations. The museum's architecture harmoniously blends modern design with ancient motifs, creating a captivating environment that reflects the profound history of the region. Its outdoor sculpture garden, adorned with works by renowned artists, offers a serene space for contemplation and reflection.

However, the highlight of the museum's collection, and indeed one of the most significant archaeological discoveries of the 20th century, is the Dead Sea Scrolls. These ancient manuscripts were found in the 1940s and 1950s in the vicinity of the Dead Sea, primarily at the archaeological site of Qumran. The scrolls date back to the Second Temple period (circa 530 BCE to 70 CE) and comprise a wide range of texts, including fragments of the Hebrew Bible, religious writings, hymns, and sectarian documents.

The discovery of the Dead Sea Scrolls has had a profound impact on biblical scholarship, religious studies, and our understanding of the ancient world. The scrolls provide invaluable insights into the development of Jewish religious thought and shed light on the historical context of the emergence of Christianity. They offer glimpses into the lives and beliefs of a Jewish sect that likely resided in the vicinity of Qumran.

The Israel Museum houses one of the most extensive collections of Dead Sea Scrolls in the world. The Shrine of the Book, an iconic structure within the museum, is dedicated to the preservation and display of these ancient manuscripts. The shrine's unique design resembles the lid of one of the clay jars in which the scrolls were discovered. The display within the shrine includes several original scrolls and fragments, offering visitors an opportunity to marvel at these ancient texts firsthand.

The Dead Sea Scrolls exhibit at the Israel Museum takes visitors on a captivating journey through time. In addition to the actual scrolls, the exhibit showcases related artifacts, such as ancient coins, pottery, and other archaeological finds from the Qumran site. Interactive displays and multimedia presentations provide context and elucidate the historical significance of the scrolls. Visitors can also explore digital reconstructions of the scrolls, which offer enhanced readability and insights into their content.

Beyond the cultural and historical significance of the Dead Sea Scrolls, their preservation and study have posed significant challenges. Due to their fragility and sensitivity to light, the scrolls are carefully conserved to ensure their long-term survival. The Israel Antiquities Authority, in collaboration with the Israel Museum, employs advanced technologies and meticulous preservation techniques to safeguard these invaluable treasures.

The Israel Museum and the Dead Sea Scrolls exhibit in Jerusalem are not only of immense scholarly importance but also offer a profound experience for visitors from all walks of life. They allow us to connect with our shared human heritage and gain a deeper appreciation for the religious, cultural, and intellectual traditions that have shaped our world. The museum's dedication to research, education, and public engagement ensures that the legacy of the Dead Sea Scrolls continues to inspire and enlighten generations to come.

MAHANE YEHUDA MARKET

Mahane Yehuda Market, also known as "The Shuk," is a vibrant and bustling marketplace located in the heart of Jerusalem, Israel. It is a renowned landmark and a significant cultural hub in the city, attracting both locals and tourists alike. With its rich history, lively atmosphere, and diverse array of goods and flavors, Mahane Yehuda

Market offers a unique and immersive experience for visitors.

The market has a long and fascinating history that dates back to the late 19th century. It began as a small, humble collection of stalls and pushcarts, serving the local Jewish community in the surrounding neighborhoods. Over time, the market grew and transformed into a vibrant commercial center, reflecting the cultural diversity and entrepreneurial spirit of Jerusalem.

Today, Mahane Yehuda Market spans over several blocks and comprises hundreds of stalls, shops, and eateries. As you navigate through its narrow alleyways, you'll find a plethora of goods, ranging from fresh fruits and vegetables to aromatic spices, from delicious baked goods to mouthwatering cheeses, and from traditional clothing to modern accessories. The market is known for its high-quality produce, and many locals come here to do their daily shopping.

Beyond the enticing array of goods, what truly sets Mahane Yehuda Market apart is its lively and energetic atmosphere. The market is always bustling with activity, especially on Fridays when locals rush to buy their provisions for the Sabbath. The sounds of vendors shouting their wares, the vibrant colors of the stalls, and the enticing aromas wafting through the air create an unforgettable sensory experience.

In recent years, Mahane Yehuda Market has undergone a revitalization, with a blend of traditional and modern elements. While it still retains its authentic charm, the market has also embraced contemporary trends and attracts a younger crowd. You'll find trendy cafes, hip bars, and stylish boutiques alongside traditional food stalls, creating a unique fusion of old and new.

One of the highlights of visiting Mahane Yehuda Market is the opportunity to savor the diverse culinary delights it has to offer. From authentic Middle Eastern dishes like falafel, hummus, and shawarma to international cuisines such as Italian, Asian, and Ethiopian, there is something to satisfy every palate. Many of the market's eateries are renowned for their quality and innovation, making it a haven for food lovers.

In addition to the gastronomic experiences, Mahane Yehuda Market also hosts various cultural events and festivals throughout the year. From live music performances to art exhibitions, these events add an extra layer of vibrancy and entertainment to the market. The market truly comes alive during festivals like "Machane Yehuda Shuk Night" and "Beer Bazaar," where the entire area transforms into a lively celebration of food, music, and culture.

Beyond its commercial and cultural significance, Mahane Yehuda Market holds a special place in the hearts of the people of Jerusalem. It serves as a meeting point for friends and families, a gathering spot for locals to connect and share stories, and a symbol of the city's resilience and unity.

In conclusion, Mahane Yehuda Market is an essential destination for anyone visiting Jerusalem. It offers an authentic and immersive experience, where you can explore the rich tapestry of flavors, sights, and sounds that make up the city's vibrant cultural fabric. Whether you're a food lover, a history enthusiast, or simply looking to soak up the lively atmosphere, a visit to Mahane Yehuda Market is an absolute must.

MOUNT ZION AND THE LAST SUPPER ROOM

Mount Zion and the Last Supper Room in Jerusalem hold immense historical and religious significance for millions of people around the world. Located within the ancient walls of the Old City, these sites are revered by Jews, Christians, and Muslims alike.

Mount Zion, also known as the City of David, is a prominent hill located just outside the southwestern corner of the Old City. It has a rich history dating back thousands of years and is mentioned several times in the Hebrew Bible. In Jewish tradition, Mount Zion is believed to be the place where King David established his capital and where the Ark of the Covenant was kept.

For Christians, Mount Zion holds special importance as the location of the Last Supper, the event commemorated in the New Testament as Jesus' final meal with his disciples before his crucifixion. The Last Supper is a significant event in Christian theology, as it is believed to be the institution of the Eucharist or Holy Communion.

The Last Supper Room, also known as the Cenacle or Upper Room, is situated on the second floor of a building on Mount Zion. It is traditionally considered to be the place where Jesus and his disciples gathered for the Last Supper. The room is rectangular in shape, with stone walls and a vaulted ceiling. It has been a site of pilgrimage for centuries, attracting countless visitors seeking to connect with the sacred events that took place there.

The Last Supper Room has witnessed various historical and religious milestones over the centuries. After the crucifixion and resurrection of Jesus, it is believed that the room served as a meeting place for the early Christian community. According to the New Testament, it was in this room that the Holy Spirit descended upon the disciples on the day of Pentecost, marking the birth of the Christian Church.

Over the centuries, the ownership and control of the Last Supper Room have changed hands numerous times. Different religious groups and empires have sought to claim and control the site. Today, the room is administered by the Franciscan Custody of the Holy Land, an order within the Roman Catholic Church, who manage and maintain the site as a place of worship and pilgrimage.

Visiting the Last Supper Room is a powerful experience for believers and non-believers alike. The room itself is adorned with religious artwork and symbols, and visitors can explore the space and contemplate the events that transpired there. Many find solace and spiritual connection in this sacred space, as it represents a pivotal moment in Christian history and the foundation of the Eucharist, one of the central sacraments of Christianity.

In addition to its religious significance, Mount Zion also has other notable sites of interest. One such site is the Church of the Dormition, a beautiful Byzantine-style church that commemorates the Assumption of Mary, the mother of Jesus, into heaven. The church's architecture, artwork, and serene atmosphere make it a popular destination for visitors.

Furthermore, adjacent to the Last Supper Room is the Tomb of David, which is considered a holy site for Jews. According to Jewish tradition, this is the burial place of King David, who is revered as one of the greatest kings in ancient Israelite history.

Mount Zion and the Last Supper Room in Jerusalem hold tremendous religious and historical significance. They serve as places of pilgrimage, prayer, and contemplation for individuals from diverse faith backgrounds. These sites offer a unique opportunity to connect with the events of the past and the enduring spiritual traditions that have shaped human civilization.

AL-AQSA MOSQUE AND THE DOME OF THE ROCK

The Al-Aqsa Mosque and the Dome of the Rock are two iconic and historically significant structures located within the Old City of Jerusalem. They hold immense religious, cultural, and architectural importance for Muslims around the world, as well as a significant place in the history of Jerusalem and the Abrahamic faiths.

The Al-Aqsa Mosque, meaning "the farthest mosque" in Arabic, is the third holiest site in Islam. It is situated on the Temple Mount, which is also revered as a sacred site in Judaism and Christianity. Muslims believe that the Prophet Muhammad traveled from Mecca to Jerusalem during the Night Journey, where he ascended to the heavens to receive revelations from God.

The Al-Aqsa Mosque is believed to be the location where the Prophet Muhammad led prayers with other prophets and messengers of God. The mosque itself has a rich history and has undergone several expansions and renovations over the centuries.

The Dome of the Rock, located adjacent to the Al-Aqsa Mosque, is an architectural masterpiece and one of the most recognizable landmarks in Jerusalem. Built in the late 7th century, it is a prime example of early Islamic architecture and has a distinct golden dome that has become an iconic symbol of Jerusalem. The Dome of the Rock holds immense significance in Islam as it is believed to be the place from which the Prophet Muhammad ascended to heaven during the Night Journey. It is also believed to be the site of the Second Jewish Temple, making it significant for both Muslims and Jews.

The architecture of the Dome of the Rock is awe-inspiring. The exterior of the structure is adorned with intricate tile work, calligraphy, and geometric patterns, reflecting the artistic and architectural traditions of the time. The interior of the dome features a stunning blend of colorful mosaics, marble columns, and a central rock, known as the Foundation Stone, which is believed to be the spot from which the world was created.

Both the Al-Aqsa Mosque and the Dome of the Rock have witnessed a turbulent history due to their strategic and religious importance. They have been the subject of various conflicts and disputes throughout the centuries, with different religious and political groups vying for control over the site. The city of Jerusalem has seen numerous conquests and changes in rulership, and the fate of these holy structures has often been intertwined with the broader political dynamics of the region.

In the modern era, the Al-Aqsa Mosque and the Dome of the Rock continue to be at the center of the Israeli-Palestinian conflict, as the status of Jerusalem remains a contentious issue. The area surrounding the Temple Mount, where these structures are located, is a source of tension between Israelis and Palestinians, with both sides claiming it as their own. The management and access to the site are subject to complex arrangements, with the Jordanian government playing a significant role in the administration of the Islamic holy sites in Jerusalem.

Despite the challenges and conflicts surrounding the Al-Aqsa Mosque and the Dome of the Rock, these structures remain cherished symbols of faith, history, and identity for Muslims worldwide. They attract millions of visitors each year, who come to pray, learn, and appreciate the remarkable architectural and spiritual legacy that they represent. Their presence in the heart of Jerusalem serves as a reminder of the city's rich and diverse history and the need for peaceful coexistence and respect among different religious and cultural communities.

CHAPTER THREE: NEIGHBORHOODS AND DISTRICTS

DOWNTOWN (CITY CENTER)

Downtown Jerusalem, also known as the City Center, is a vibrant and historically significant area located in the heart of Jerusalem, Israel. Steeped in rich culture and religious significance, Downtown Jerusalem is a captivating blend of ancient landmarks, modern development, bustling markets, and a thriving urban atmosphere. As the commercial, cultural, and political hub of the city, Downtown Jerusalem offers a unique and unforgettable experience for visitors and locals alike.

One of the defining features of Downtown Jerusalem is its historical importance. The area is home to some of the most sacred sites in Judaism, Christianity, and Islam, making it a significant pilgrimage destination for followers of these faiths. The Western Wall, also known as the Wailing Wall, is a remnant of the ancient Jewish temple and is one of the most revered sites in Judaism. Thousands of visitors come here daily to pray, reflect, and place notes in the cracks of the wall.

Another iconic religious site in Downtown Jerusalem is the Church of the Holy Sepulchre. This revered Christian pilgrimage site is believed to be the location of Jesus' crucifixion, burial, and resurrection. The church is a stunning example of medieval architecture and contains several chapels and shrines commemorating different events in Jesus' life.

The Dome of the Rock, an iconic golden-domed structure, stands atop the Temple Mount and is one of the most recognizable symbols of Jerusalem. It is a significant site in Islam and holds religious importance for Muslims worldwide. While non-Muslims are not permitted inside the mosque, the exterior and the surrounding plaza are worth exploring for their architectural grandeur and historical significance.

In addition to its religious landmarks, Downtown Jerusalem offers a diverse range of cultural attractions. The bustling Machane Yehuda Market, commonly referred to as "The Shuk," is a vibrant and colorful market where locals and tourists converge to shop for fresh produce, spices, baked goods, and a variety of other products. The market is a feast for the senses, with its aromatic spices, lively atmosphere, and bustling energy.

Beyond the religious and cultural sites, Downtown Jerusalem is also a thriving modern center with a wide array of shops, boutiques, cafes, restaurants, and entertainment venues. Ben Yehuda Street, a pedestrianized thoroughfare, is a bustling hub of activity, filled with street performers, vendors, and shops selling everything from souvenirs to designer clothing. The street comes alive at night, with lively bars and restaurants offering a vibrant nightlife scene.

Downtown Jerusalem also serves as the political center of Israel, housing important government buildings and institutions. The Knesset, Israel's parliament, is located in the city center and is a symbol of Israeli democracy. Visitors can tour the Knesset and learn about the country's political system and history.

The beauty of Downtown Jerusalem lies in its ability to seamlessly blend ancient traditions with modern life. The juxtaposition of ancient religious sites with contemporary cafes and shops creates a unique and dynamic atmosphere. Whether strolling through the narrow alleyways of the Old City, exploring the bustling markets, or enjoying the vibrant street life, Downtown Jerusalem offers an experience that is both spiritually uplifting and culturally enriching.

It's important to note that Jerusalem, including Downtown, is a city of great significance and sensitivity for various religious and political reasons. It is essential for visitors to respect the diverse religious and cultural traditions while exploring this remarkable city.

In conclusion, Downtown Jerusalem, with its historical landmarks, religious sites, vibrant markets, and modern developments, is a captivating destination that holds immense cultural, religious, and historical significance. It is a place where ancient traditions converge with contemporary life, creating a unique and unforgettable experience for all who visit.

MAMILLA AND BEN YEHUDA STREET

Mamilla and Ben Yehuda Street are two iconic locations in Jerusalem, Israel, that hold significant historical, cultural, and commercial importance. They are bustling streets that attract locals and tourists alike, offering a vibrant atmosphere and a unique blend of modernity and tradition.

Mamilla, also known as Mamilla Mall or Alrov Mamilla Avenue, is a pedestrianized promenade located just outside the walls of the Old City of Jerusalem. It stretches from the Jaffa Gate to the upscale Mamilla neighborhood. Mamilla has a rich history that dates back thousands of years. In ancient times, it served as a vital gateway to the Old City. The street was home to various civilizations, including the Canaanites, Romans, and Byzantines, and witnessed numerous significant events throughout history.

In recent years, Mamilla has undergone extensive redevelopment, transforming it into a luxurious shopping and entertainment destination. The modern Mamilla Mall offers a diverse range of high-end boutiques, designer stores, international brands, and exquisite restaurants. The architecture seamlessly blends the old and the new, with renovated historic buildings standing alongside contemporary structures. Mamilla also features several luxury hotels, providing visitors with a stylish and convenient place to stay.

Beyond its commercial offerings, Mamilla is also renowned for its cultural attractions. The street is lined with art galleries, showcasing both local and international works, and it frequently hosts art exhibitions and cultural events. Additionally, Mamilla boasts several upscale bars and cafes, making it a popular spot for locals and tourists to socialize and enjoy a vibrant nightlife.

Moving on to Ben Yehuda Street, it is one of the most famous and vibrant pedestrian streets in Jerusalem. Located in the heart of the city, it stretches from Zion Square to Jaffa Street. Ben Yehuda Street has long been a focal point for locals and tourists, offering a wide range of shops, cafes, street performers, and cultural experiences.

Named after the influential Zionist leader, Eliezer Ben-Yehuda, who played a vital role in the revival of the Hebrew language, Ben Yehuda Street has a lively and energetic atmosphere. The street is known for its bustling outdoor market, where vendors sell a variety of goods, including clothing, souvenirs, jewelry, and traditional Middle Eastern products. The market's lively ambiance, coupled with the scent of fresh spices and the sounds of bargaining, create a truly authentic experience.

Ben Yehuda Street is also famous for its diverse culinary scene. It is home to numerous cafes, restaurants, and food stalls, offering a wide array of cuisine options, ranging from traditional Israeli dishes to international flavors. Whether it's enjoying a cup of coffee while people-watching, savoring local delicacies, or trying street food favorites, Ben Yehuda Street provides a culinary adventure for every taste.

Furthermore, Ben Yehuda Street serves as a hub for cultural events and street performances. Musicians, street artists, and entertainers fill the air with their talents, creating a vibrant and dynamic ambiance.

Visitors can witness live music performances, dance shows, and even join impromptu celebrations, especially during holidays and festivals.

Both Mamilla and Ben Yehuda Street contribute to Jerusalem's unique charm and allure. They are emblematic of the city's rich history, cultural diversity, and vibrant lifestyle. These bustling streets offer a delightful blend of ancient and modern experiences, attracting visitors from around the world and serving as cherished gathering places for locals. Whether one seeks luxury shopping, cultural exploration, culinary delights, or simply soaking in the lively atmosphere, Mamilla and Ben Yehuda Street are must-visit destinations that showcase the essence of Jerusalem.

EIN KAREM

Ein Karem, located on the western outskirts of Jerusalem, is a picturesque and historic neighborhood that holds immense cultural, religious, and natural significance. This charming village has a rich history dating back thousands of years, making it a popular destination for locals and tourists alike.

The name "Ein Karem" means "Spring of the Vineyard" in Hebrew, which aptly describes the lush and fertile landscape surrounding the area. The village is nestled within the verdant hills of the Jerusalem Forest, offering stunning views and a tranquil atmosphere. The combination of natural beauty and historical importance has earned

Ein Karem its reputation as a gem of Jerusalem.

One of the most significant aspects of Ein Karem is its association with biblical narratives. According to Christian tradition, Ein Karem is believed to be the birthplace of John the Baptist. It is said that John's parents, Elizabeth and Zacharias, resided in Ein Karem, and it was here that Mary, the mother of Jesus, visited her cousin Elizabeth during her pregnancy. The meeting between Mary and Elizabeth, known as the Visitation, is commemorated by the Church of the Visitation, a prominent landmark in Ein Karem.

The Church of the Visitation is a magnificent structure that stands on the site where Elizabeth is said to have greeted Mary. The church features stunning architectural elements and beautiful artwork, including a marble sculpture of the Visitation scene. Pilgrims from all over the world visit this church to pay homage to the biblical event and to soak in the spiritual atmosphere.

Another notable religious site in Ein Karem is the Church of St. John the Baptist, located near the spring that gives the village its name. This ancient church is believed to be built on the spot where John the Baptist was born. It showcases an array of architectural styles, ranging from Crusader to Byzantine, and contains fascinating archaeological remains, including a mosaic floor from the Byzantine era.

Apart from its religious significance, Ein Karem is also renowned for its artistic and cultural heritage. The village has long been a haven for artists, musicians, and writers who draw inspiration from its serene surroundings. The narrow streets are lined with charming stone houses adorned with vibrant flowers and artistic decorations. Numerous art galleries and studios showcase the works of local artists, adding to the creative ambiance of the village.

In addition to its historical and cultural attractions, Ein Karem offers visitors an opportunity to explore the natural beauty of the region. The surrounding hills provide excellent hiking trails, allowing visitors to enjoy breathtaking views of the landscape, dotted with olive groves and vineyards. The combination of the rolling hills, ancient trees, and the gentle sound of flowing water from the springs creates a soothing and idyllic setting.

Ein Karem is also known for its culinary delights, with a variety of charming cafes and restaurants serving traditional Middle Eastern cuisine. Visitors can indulge in mouthwatering dishes while enjoying the peaceful atmosphere and the warm hospitality of the locals.

In conclusion, Ein Karem is a captivating neighborhood that encapsulates the essence of Jerusalem's rich history, religious heritage, artistic spirit, and natural beauty. Whether you are interested in exploring the biblical narratives, admiring artistic creations, immersing yourself in nature, or simply seeking a place of tranquility, Ein Karem offers a unique and memorable experience. It is a testament to the enduring cultural tapestry of Jerusalem and a must-visit destination for anyone traveling to this remarkable city.

MEA SHEARIM

Mea Shearim is an iconic and deeply traditional neighborhood located in the heart of Jerusalem, Israel. Known for its ultra-Orthodox Jewish population, Mea Shearim is a fascinating enclave that offers a glimpse into a bygone era. Stepping into this neighborhood is like stepping back in time, as its inhabitants strive to maintain a way of life that is rooted in centuries-old traditions.

The history of Mea Shearim dates back to the late 19th century when it was established as one of the first Jewish neighborhoods outside the walls of the Old City. The neighborhood's name, which means "one hundred gates" in Hebrew, was inspired by the verse in Genesis that describes the blessings Jacob bestowed upon his son Judah.

The residents of Mea Shearim belong to various Hasidic and Haredi sects, including Satmar, Ger, Belz, and many others. These groups adhere strictly to traditional Jewish practices, emphasizing religious observance, modesty, and separation from secular influences. The community in Mea Shearim is deeply committed to preserving its unique cultural and religious heritage, which shapes every aspect of daily life.

Walking through the narrow streets of Mea Shearim, one encounters a distinct atmosphere. Men dressed in long black coats and wide-brimmed hats rush to their daily prayers at the neighborhood's numerous synagogues. Women wear modest clothing, often donning head scarves or wigs as a sign of marital modesty. The streets are filled with bustling activity, as shopkeepers sell religious items, kosher food, and traditional clothing.

One of the most striking aspects of Mea Shearim is the strict separation between men and women. In certain areas, men and women walk on separate sides of the street, ensuring minimal interaction between the genders. This separation extends to public transportation as well, with segregated seating on buses and separate entrances for men and women.

The architecture of Mea Shearim is also unique, reflecting the traditional style prevalent during its establishment. The buildings are constructed with a distinctive Jerusalem stone and adorned with ornate balconies and intricate facades. These structures, often several stories high, house large extended families, with generations living under one roof.

Despite its traditionalism, Mea Shearim has not remained completely isolated from the modern world. Some residents have embraced technology to a limited extent, using smartphones and computers for business purposes while still adhering to strict guidelines to avoid any potential negative influences. However, the influence of the outside world is generally minimized, as the community maintains its insularity and self-sufficiency.

While the residents of Mea Shearim primarily focus on their religious studies and observance, they are also known for their activism and efforts to preserve their way of life. They have been active in resisting attempts to enforce more secular practices in the neighborhood, such as the opening of businesses on the Sabbath or the introduction of immodest dress in public spaces.

Visitors to Mea Shearim are advised to dress modestly and respect the residents' customs and sensitivities. It is crucial to refrain from taking photographs without permission, as many residents consider it a violation of their religious beliefs. The neighborhood offers guided tours that provide an opportunity to learn about the community's history, traditions, and way of life directly from its residents.

Mea Shearim stands as a testament to the enduring strength of Jewish tradition and the power of community. Its residents, through their unwavering commitment to their faith and cultural heritage, have preserved a unique enclave within one of the world's most historic and diverse cities. As Jerusalem continues to evolve, Mea Shearim remains a captivating and authentic glimpse into a way of life deeply rooted in the past.

MACHANE YEHUDA AND NACHLAOT

Machane Yehuda and Nachlaot are two vibrant and culturally rich neighborhoods located in Jerusalem, Israel. Each with its distinct character and history, these areas offer visitors and residents alike a unique and immersive experience.

Let's start with Machane Yehuda, also known as "the Shuk." It is one of Jerusalem's most famous open-air markets, bustling with activity and renowned for its lively atmosphere. The market stretches across several blocks, and its narrow alleys are lined with an array of vendors selling a wide variety of goods. From fresh fruits and vegetables to aromatic spices, baked goods, dairy products, and traditional Middle Eastern delicacies, the Shuk is a paradise for food lovers and culinary enthusiasts.

Machane Yehuda is not just a place to buy groceries; it's a cultural hub that reflects the diversity and vibrancy of Jerusalem. As you explore the market, you'll encounter a melting pot of people from different backgrounds, religions, and nationalities. The sounds of merchants calling out their goods, the aromas wafting through the air, and the colorful displays of produce create a sensory experience like no other.

Beyond its culinary delights, Machane Yehuda has also undergone significant revitalization in recent years. The market has transformed into a trendy hotspot, attracting both locals and tourists. The narrow lanes that were once solely dedicated to produce stalls now house an eclectic mix of trendy bars, restaurants, and boutique shops. In the evening, the Shuk comes alive with vibrant nightlife, where visitors can enjoy live music performances, sip on cocktails, and indulge in a diverse range of cuisines.

Adjacent to Machane Yehuda lies the enchanting neighborhood of Nachlaot. Known for its charming architecture and bohemian atmosphere, Nachlaot offers a glimpse into the city's past. This historic neighborhood is made up of a maze of narrow streets and alleyways, each with its own unique character. The buildings, adorned with intricate details and colorful facades, showcase the architectural styles of Jerusalem's diverse communities.

Nachlaot is a neighborhood deeply rooted in tradition and religious significance. It is home to a mix of religious and secular residents, creating a harmonious blend of ancient and modern Jerusalem. Walking through Nachlaot, you'll encounter synagogues, small courtyards known as "makolets," and community centers where locals gather to socialize and celebrate.

Beyond its historical significance, Nachlaot has become an attractive destination for artists, musicians, and creative individuals. The neighborhood is dotted with art galleries, studios, and performance spaces, showcasing the vibrant artistic scene of Jerusalem. Visitors can browse through unique artworks, attend live music concerts, or even participate in workshops to explore their creative side.

Both Machane Yehuda and Nachlaot reflect the dynamism and diversity of Jerusalem. They encapsulate the city's rich history, multiculturalism, and the fusion of old and new. Together, these neighborhoods offer a sensory and immersive experience, inviting visitors to savor the flavors, engage with the local community, and explore the artistic and cultural tapestry of Jerusalem. Whether you're a food lover, a history enthusiast, or an art connoisseur, Machane Yehuda and Nachlaot are must-visit destinations that will leave a lasting impression on your journey through Jerusalem.

CHAPTER FOUR: MUSEUMS AND CULTURAL INSTITUTIONS

ISRAEL MUSEUM

The Israel Museum in Jerusalem is a remarkable cultural institution that stands as a testament to the rich history, diverse heritage, and artistic brilliance of the region. Established in 1965, the museum has grown to become one of the world's leading centers for art, archaeology, and Jewish culture.

Situated in the heart of Jerusalem, the Israel Museum is located on a sprawling 20-acre campus that offers a captivating journey through time and space. The museum's collections span a vast range of periods and civilizations, housing artifacts from ancient

Israel, the Middle East, and beyond. It serves as a bridge between the past and present, offering visitors an immersive experience into the heritage and artistic achievements of various civilizations.

The museum's most renowned attraction is the Shrine of the Book, which houses the Dead Sea Scrolls. These ancient manuscripts, discovered in the mid-20th century in the caves of Qumran, provide invaluable insights into the religious and historical context of the Second Temple period. The Shrine of the Book's unique architectural design, resembling the lids of the clay jars in which the scrolls were found, adds to the mystical ambiance and reverence surrounding these ancient texts.

Another notable feature of the Israel Museum is the expansive Billy Rose Art Garden. Designed by Japanese-American sculptor Isamu Noguchi, this serene outdoor space seamlessly blends nature, art, and architecture. The garden features an array of sculptures and installations, including works by renowned artists such as Pablo Picasso and Auguste Rodin. The harmonious integration of art and nature creates a contemplative environment, inviting visitors to reflect and engage with the artworks in a tranquil setting.

Inside the museum's galleries, visitors can explore an impressive collection of art and archaeological treasures. The Samuel and Saidye Bronfman Archaeology Wing offers a comprehensive display of ancient artifacts, showcasing the material culture of various civilizations that once thrived in the region. From Egyptian mummies and Canaanite pottery to Roman statues and Byzantine jewelry, the exhibits provide a captivating journey through millennia of human history.

The museum's Fine Arts Wing hosts a diverse range of artworks spanning from classical to contemporary. The European art collection boasts masterpieces by renowned artists such as Rembrandt, Monet, and Van Gogh, while the modern and contemporary art section showcases the works of Israeli and international artists. The visual richness and cultural diversity of the collection make it a must-visit destination for art enthusiasts from around the world.

In addition to its permanent collections, the Israel Museum regularly hosts temporary exhibitions that explore various themes, artists, and historical periods. These exhibitions bring a dynamic element to the museum, offering fresh perspectives and engaging narratives that complement the permanent displays. From photography and sculpture to multimedia installations and interactive displays, these temporary exhibitions provide a platform for contemporary artists to share their vision and engage with the museum's visitors.

Beyond its role as a museum, the institution serves as an educational and research center, offering a multitude of programs and resources for scholars, students, and the general public. The museum's library houses an extensive collection of books, manuscripts, and archives, catering to researchers interested in the fields of archaeology, art history, and Jewish studies. The museum also hosts lectures, workshops, and educational activities, promoting a deeper understanding and appreciation of the arts, culture, and history of the region.

The Israel Museum is not only a cultural landmark but also a symbol of coexistence and dialogue in a region often marked by conflict. It strives to foster cross-cultural understanding and bridge gaps between different communities through the universal language of art and heritage. By showcasing the diverse artistic achievements of civilizations past and present, the museum encourages visitors to explore shared human experiences and transcend the boundaries of time, place, and culture.

In conclusion, the Israel Museum in Jerusalem stands as a testament to the vibrant and multifaceted heritage of the region. Through its comprehensive collections, captivating exhibitions, and educational programs, the museum offers visitors a unique opportunity to delve into the depths of history, appreciate the beauty of art, and engage with the cultural tapestry that shapes the identity of Israel and the broader Middle East. A visit to the Israel Museum is an enriching experience that leaves a lasting impression, inviting visitors to explore the past, appreciate the present, and imagine the future.

TOWER OF DAVID MUSEUM

The Tower of David Museum, located in the historic city of Jerusalem, is a captivating cultural institution that offers visitors a unique journey through the rich and diverse history of the city. Housed within the ancient citadel known as the Tower of David, the museum is renowned for its fascinating exhibits, archaeological findings, and immersive storytelling that bring the past to life.

The Tower of David itself is a testament to Jerusalem's layered history, with construction dating back over 2,000 years. It has served various purposes throughout its existence, including as a fortress, a royal palace, a prison, and now as a site of cultural heritage and education. The museum takes full advantage of this remarkable setting, utilizing the ancient walls and structures to create a truly immersive experience for visitors.

One of the museum's highlights is its permanent exhibition, which presents the history of Jerusalem from ancient times to the modern era. Through a combination of archaeological artifacts, multimedia presentations, and interactive displays, visitors can explore the city's vibrant past, from the days of King David to the present day. The exhibition covers key historical periods, including the First and Second Temple periods, the Roman era, the Crusades, Ottoman rule, and the establishment of the State of Israel.

The Tower of David Museum also hosts temporary exhibitions that delve into specific aspects of Jerusalem's history, art, and culture. These exhibitions often showcase rare artifacts, works of art, and multimedia installations that provide unique insights into different periods and themes. From ancient archaeological treasures to contemporary artistic interpretations, these exhibitions offer a diverse range of perspectives on the city's past and present.

In addition to its exhibitions, the museum offers a range of educational programs and activities for visitors of all ages. These include guided tours, workshops, lectures, and special events that provide further opportunities for engagement and learning.

Whether you're a history enthusiast, an art lover, or simply curious about Jerusalem's heritage, the museum caters to a wide range of interests and provides a valuable educational experience.

One of the standout features of the Tower of David Museum is its spectacular panoramic view of Jerusalem from the top of the tower. Visitors can ascend to the observation deck and enjoy breathtaking vistas of the Old City, the surrounding neighborhoods, and the stunning landscape beyond. This bird's-eye view offers a unique perspective on the city's geography and serves as a reminder of Jerusalem's significance as a cultural and religious crossroads.

Moreover, the museum actively embraces technology to enhance the visitor experience. It utilizes multimedia installations, augmented reality, and virtual reality to bring historical events and sites to life. These innovative approaches provide a dynamic and engaging way to understand and connect with Jerusalem's complex past.

Beyond its historical and cultural significance, the Tower of David Museum plays a vital role in promoting dialogue and understanding among different communities in Jerusalem. It serves as a venue for various cultural events, conferences, and initiatives that aim to foster cooperation and respect among the city's diverse inhabitants. By facilitating meaningful interactions and discussions, the museum contributes to the ongoing efforts for peace, tolerance, and coexistence in Jerusalem.

In conclusion, the Tower of David Museum is a must-visit destination for anyone interested in the history, art, and culture of Jerusalem. With its extraordinary setting, comprehensive exhibitions, engaging educational programs, and commitment to fostering dialogue, the museum offers a profound and enriching experience. It stands as a beacon of knowledge, showcasing the captivating story of Jerusalem and its enduring significance as a city of immense historical and cultural importance.

BIBLE LANDS MUSEUM

The Bible Lands Museum in Jerusalem is a prominent cultural institution that offers a captivating journey through the ancient lands of the Bible. Located in the heart of Jerusalem, this museum stands as a testament to the rich history, art, and archaeology of the biblical world. With its vast collection of artifacts, interactive displays, and educational programs, the museum provides a unique opportunity for visitors to explore the fascinating heritage of the ancient Near East.

The museum was established in 1992 by Dr. Elie Borowski, an avid collector and scholar of biblical archaeology. Driven by his passion to preserve and share the treasures of the biblical lands, he created a space that would showcase the historical and cultural significance of these regions. Today, the Bible Lands Museum stands as one of the leading institutions dedicated to promoting the understanding and appreciation of the biblical world.

One of the most remarkable aspects of the Bible Lands Museum is its collection of artifacts. The museum houses a vast array of archaeological finds from Egypt, Mesopotamia, Anatolia, Persia, Greece, and, of course, the Holy Land itself. These artifacts span thousands of years, from prehistoric times to the early Christian era, providing a comprehensive overview of the civilizations that once flourished in these lands. From intricately carved statues and reliefs to delicate pottery and jewelry, each piece offers a glimpse into the lives and beliefs of ancient peoples.

The museum's exhibits are thoughtfully curated, taking visitors on a chronological and thematic journey through the ancient world. As you walk through the halls, you'll encounter displays dedicated to the art, religion, daily life, and technological advancements of various civilizations. The exhibits not only present the material culture of these ancient societies but also shed light on their social structures, religious practices, and artistic achievements. The combination of archaeological artifacts, explanatory texts, and multimedia presentations creates an immersive and engaging experience for visitors of all ages.

One of the highlights of the Bible Lands Museum is its model of ancient Jerusalem. This meticulously crafted model provides a detailed reconstruction of the city during the Second Temple period, allowing visitors to visualize the grandeur of the Temple Mount, the bustling streets, and the architectural wonders of the time. The model serves as a valuable educational tool, illustrating the biblical accounts and providing historical context for the stories and events that unfolded in Jerusalem thousands of years ago.

In addition to its permanent exhibits, the museum hosts temporary exhibitions that delve deeper into specific themes or regions.

These exhibitions often feature loans from other international institutions, offering visitors a chance to see rare and unique artifacts that are not part of the museum's regular collection. The temporary exhibitions ensure that there is always something new to discover, making each visit to the Bible Lands Museum a fresh and enriching experience.

The educational programs at the Bible Lands Museum are another integral part of its mission. The museum offers guided tours, workshops, lectures, and other activities designed to enhance visitors' understanding of the ancient world. School groups, families, and individuals can all benefit from the educational initiatives, which aim to foster a deeper appreciation for the historical and cultural heritage of the Bible lands.

Moreover, the Bible Lands Museum is committed to scholarly research and publication. Its team of archaeologists, curators, and researchers actively contribute to the field of biblical archaeology, producing academic publications, organizing conferences, and collaborating with other institutions. Through these efforts, the museum not only serves as a repository of ancient artifacts but also contributes to the advancement of knowledge in the field.

In conclusion, the Bible Lands Museum in Jerusalem is a treasure trove of history, art, and archaeology. It provides a captivating journey through the ancient lands of the Bible, showcasing the diverse civilizations that once thrived in the region. With its extensive collection, informative exhibits, and educational programs, the museum offers a unique opportunity to explore the wonders of the past and gain a deeper understanding of the biblical world. Whether you are a history enthusiast, a scholar, or simply curious about ancient civilizations, a visit to the Bible Lands Museum is a truly enriching experience.

MUSEUM OF ISLAMIC ART

The Museum of Islamic Art in Jerusalem is a renowned cultural institution that stands as a testament to the rich heritage and artistic brilliance of the Islamic world.

Situated in the heart of Jerusalem, this museum showcases a diverse collection of Islamic art and artifacts, spanning centuries and encompassing various regions.

The museum's establishment dates back to 1974 when it was founded by Professor Majed Khalaily, an avid collector and art enthusiast. His vision was to create a space dedicated to preserving and celebrating Islamic art, architecture, and culture. Today, the Museum of Islamic Art stands as a remarkable testament to his passion and dedication.

One of the standout features of the museum is its architectural brilliance. The building itself is a work of art, blending traditional Islamic architectural elements with modern design. The museum's elegant domes, intricate tile work, and beautifully landscaped courtyards create a serene and captivating atmosphere, transporting visitors into the world of Islamic art and culture.

The museum's collection is vast and diverse, featuring thousands of artifacts from across the Islamic world. Visitors can explore a wide range of art forms, including calligraphy, ceramics, textiles, metalwork, woodwork, and glasswork. Each piece is a testament to the incredible craftsmanship and artistic ingenuity that flourished throughout Islamic history.

The exhibits are thoughtfully curated, allowing visitors to embark on a chronological journey through Islamic art. Starting from the early Islamic period, the museum showcases artifacts from the Umayyad, Abbasid, and Fatimid dynasties, offering insights into the development of artistic styles and techniques over time. Visitors can marvel at intricately carved Qur'ans, delicate Persian miniatures, and exquisite Ottoman textiles, among other treasures.

In addition to its permanent collection, the Museum of Islamic Art also hosts temporary exhibitions, focusing on specific themes or artists. These exhibitions provide a dynamic and ever-evolving experience, allowing visitors to delve deeper into various aspects of Islamic art and culture.

Beyond its role as a museum, the institution serves as an educational hub, offering a range of programs and activities for visitors of all ages. Guided tours, workshops, lectures, and cultural events are regularly organized, providing opportunities for individuals to deepen their understanding and appreciation of Islamic art. The museum's educational initiatives play a vital role in promoting cross-cultural dialogue and fostering a greater understanding of the Islamic world.

The Museum of Islamic Art in Jerusalem is not only a cultural gem but also an important symbol of unity and harmony. It stands as a bridge between different cultures, religions, and civilizations, promoting tolerance and fostering a sense of shared humanity. In a city as historically significant and diverse as Jerusalem, this museum serves as a vital space for cultural exchange, encouraging dialogue and understanding among people from various backgrounds.

In conclusion, the Museum of Islamic Art in Jerusalem is a treasure trove of Islamic culture and heritage. With its stunning architecture, extensive collection, and educational initiatives, the museum offers a unique and enriching experience for visitors. It stands as a beacon of art, history, and cross-cultural understanding, contributing to the preservation and promotion of Islamic art for generations to come.

ROCKEFELLER ARCHEOLOGICAL MUSEUM

The Rockefeller Archaeological Museum, located in Jerusalem, is a prominent institution dedicated to the preservation and exhibition of archaeological artifacts and cultural heritage in the region. Named after its benefactor, American industrialist and philanthropist John D. Rockefeller Jr., the museum has played a vital role in the understanding and appreciation of the rich history of Jerusalem and the surrounding areas.

The museum was established in 1938 and is situated in a stunning building that blends architectural styles from the Byzantine, Arab, and Crusader periods. Designed by renowned architect Austin St. Barbe Harrison, the museum's structure itself is a testament to the cultural significance of Jerusalem and its historical layers.

The Rockefeller Archaeological Museum houses a vast collection of archaeological finds, primarily from Jerusalem and its environs. The exhibits cover a wide range of periods, from prehistoric times to the Ottoman era. The artifacts on display offer insights into the diverse civilizations that have thrived in the region, including Canaanite, Israelite, Hellenistic, Roman, Byzantine, Islamic, and Crusader cultures.

One of the most noteworthy exhibits in the museum is the renowned Model of Jerusalem in the Second Temple Period.

Created by the British archaeologist Conrad Schick in the late 19th century, the 1:50 scale model meticulously depicts the city during the time of Herod the Great. It provides visitors with a comprehensive view of the architecture, urban planning, and topography of Jerusalem in this significant historical era.

Additionally, the Rockefeller Archaeological Museum boasts an extensive collection of ancient pottery, jewelry, coins, and other artifacts that shed light on the daily lives, beliefs, and artistic achievements of the various civilizations that inhabited the region throughout history. The museum's exhibits are accompanied by informative labels and multimedia presentations that enhance the visitor's understanding of the artifacts' historical and cultural contexts.

Beyond its role as a museum, the Rockefeller Archaeological Museum has served as an important center for archaeological research and conservation. The museum houses a library and archives that are accessible to scholars and researchers interested in delving deeper into the rich archaeological heritage of the area.

The museum's location in Jerusalem holds special significance due to the city's historical and cultural importance. It is strategically situated near significant archaeological sites, such as the Temple Mount, the City of David, and the Western Wall. This proximity allows visitors to explore the museum's exhibits in conjunction with their visits to these iconic sites, providing a comprehensive understanding of Jerusalem's past.

Over the years, the Rockefeller Archaeological Museum has undergone various renovations and expansions to improve its facilities and enhance its exhibition spaces. These efforts have allowed for the presentation of artifacts in a modern and engaging manner, offering visitors a dynamic and immersive experience.

In conclusion, the Rockefeller Archaeological Museum in Jerusalem stands as a beacon of archaeological preservation, research, and education. Through its extensive collection and thoughtful exhibits, it provides a window into the rich and diverse history of the region. The museum's commitment to sharing knowledge and promoting cultural understanding makes it a vital institution in preserving and celebrating Jerusalem's heritage for generations to come.

BLOOMFIELD SCIENCE MUSEUM

The Bloomfield Science Museum, located in Jerusalem, is a captivating and educational institution that brings science and technology to life. Established in 1992, the museum has become a popular destination for locals and tourists alike, offering a wide range of interactive exhibits, hands-on activities, and educational programs. With its commitment to fostering curiosity, exploration, and learning, the Bloomfield Science Museum serves as a hub for scientific discovery and innovation in the heart of Jerusalem.

Exhibits and Interactive Displays:

The museum boasts a diverse array of exhibits, each designed to engage visitors of all ages and interests. The exhibits cover various scientific disciplines, including physics, biology, chemistry, space exploration, and more. One of the museum's most prominent features is its emphasis on interactive displays, enabling visitors to actively participate and engage with the concepts being presented.

For instance, the "Science Park" section offers a range of interactive exhibits that demonstrate scientific principles in a playful and engaging manner. Visitors can explore the properties of water, witness the power of electricity, experience the wonders of optics, and even discover the secrets of human perception. These hands-on exhibits encourage visitors to touch, experiment, and explore, promoting a deeper understanding and appreciation for scientific phenomena.

Additionally, the museum hosts temporary exhibitions that delve into specific scientific topics or showcase groundbreaking research. These exhibitions provide visitors with a glimpse into the latest scientific advancements and encourage critical thinking and curiosity.

Education and Outreach:

The Bloomfield Science Museum is dedicated to promoting scientific literacy and education. It offers a wide range of educational programs and activities catering to various age groups, from preschoolers to adults. The museum's educational initiatives aim to make science accessible, engaging, and relevant to people from all backgrounds.

For school groups, the museum offers tailored programs that align with the Israeli national curriculum, providing students with hands-on experiences that complement classroom learning. These programs foster a love for science, encourage inquiry-based learning, and inspire future generations of scientists, engineers, and innovators.

The museum also organizes workshops, lectures, and demonstrations for visitors of all ages. These events feature scientists, researchers, and experts who share their knowledge and insights on diverse scientific topics. By providing access to experts in the field, the museum fosters a culture of lifelong learning and encourages visitors to explore science beyond the museum's walls.

Community Engagement and Impact:
The Bloomfield Science Museum actively engages with the local community, working to bridge gaps in scientific education and promote inclusivity. It collaborates with schools, community centers, and

organizations to bring science to underserved populations, ensuring that everyone has the opportunity to experience the wonders of science and technology.

Furthermore, the museum hosts special events and activities during holidays and festivals, attracting families and creating a vibrant atmosphere. These events often feature interactive shows, demonstrations, and hands-on activities, sparking the curiosity of visitors of all ages and backgrounds.

In a nutshell, the Bloomfield Science Museum in Jerusalem stands as a beacon of scientific exploration and education. Through its engaging exhibits, interactive displays, educational programs, and community outreach efforts, the museum fosters a love for science and technology, inspiring visitors to explore, discover, and embrace the wonders of the natural world. Whether you are a student, a curious individual, or a family seeking a captivating and educational experience, the Bloomfield Science Museum offers a journey of discovery that is both entertaining and enlightening.

L.A. MAYER MUSEUM FOR ISLAMIC ART

The L.A. Mayer Museum for Islamic Art in Jerusalem is a prestigious cultural institution that serves as a testament to the rich and diverse heritage of Islamic art and culture. Located in the heart of Jerusalem, this museum showcases an extensive collection of Islamic art, artifacts, and historical objects, making it a significant destination for art enthusiasts, scholars, and visitors from around the world.

The museum was established in 1974 and named after its founder, Sir David Lionel Abrahams Mayer, who was an avid collector of Islamic art. Mayer's passion for Islamic art led him to amass a remarkable collection of over 5,000 items, including textiles, ceramics, metalwork, jewelry, manuscripts, and carpets, spanning over a thousand years of Islamic history.

The architecture of the L.A. Mayer Museum is a captivating blend of modern and traditional styles, designed to harmonize with the surrounding landscape and reflect the essence of Islamic aesthetics. The museum building itself is an architectural gem, featuring elegant domes, arches, and courtyards that evoke the grandeur of Islamic architectural traditions.

Upon entering the museum, visitors are greeted by a vast display of stunning Islamic calligraphy, which serves as an introduction to the art of the written word in Islamic culture. The collection encompasses beautifully illuminated Qur'ans, calligraphic panels, and manuscripts that showcase the intricate mastery of Islamic calligraphers throughout the centuries.

Moving through the museum's galleries, visitors are immersed in the diverse artistic traditions of the Islamic world. The exhibits are thoughtfully curated to highlight the different periods, regions, and mediums of Islamic art, providing an insightful journey through time and space.

One can explore the mesmerizing beauty of Islamic ceramics, including exquisite tiles, vessels, and decorative objects. These ceramics showcase the intricate patterns, vibrant colors, and technical sophistication that have become synonymous with Islamic art. The museum's collection includes notable pieces from various centers of ceramic production, such as Iznik in Turkey, Kashan in Iran, and Damascus in Syria.

The L.A. Mayer Museum also boasts an impressive collection of textiles, including woven fabrics, carpets, and embroideries. These textiles exemplify the mastery of Islamic weavers and craftsmen, featuring intricate designs, rich colors, and exquisite techniques. The collection encompasses textiles from different regions, including Persia, Central Asia, and Andalusia, providing a glimpse into the diversity and evolution of Islamic textile art.

In addition to ceramics and textiles, the museum houses an array of metalwork, jewelry, and woodwork. Visitors can marvel at finely crafted metal objects, such as ornate bowls, candlesticks, and weaponry. The jewelry collection showcases intricate designs adorned with precious gemstones, reflecting the Islamic fascination with beauty and adornment. The woodwork collection includes intricately carved architectural elements, furniture, and decorative objects that display the skill and artistry of Islamic woodworkers.

Beyond the physical artifacts, the L.A. Mayer Museum offers a comprehensive educational experience. It hosts temporary exhibitions, lectures, and workshops that delve deeper into various aspects of Islamic art, culture, and history. The museum's educational programs aim to foster understanding, appreciation, and dialogue, bridging the gap between different cultures and promoting intercultural exchange.

Furthermore, the L.A. Mayer Museum is committed to research and scholarship in the field of Islamic art. It houses an extensive library and archives that provide resources for researchers, scholars, and students interested in delving into the intricacies of Islamic art and culture.

In conclusion, the L.A. Mayer Museum for Islamic Art in Jerusalem stands as a testament to the richness, diversity, and beauty of Islamic art. Its remarkable collection, breathtaking architecture, and commitment to education and research make it a true cultural gem. The museum serves as a bridge between civilizations, promoting cross-cultural understanding and appreciation, and is an essential destination for anyone seeking to explore the vibrant world of Islamic art.

CHAPTER FIVE: PRACTICAL INFORMATION

CURRENCY, BANKING, AND ATMs

Jerusalem offers a well-established banking system, a wide range of currency options, and an extensive network of ATMs (Automated Teller Machines). In this note, we will delve into the details of currency, banking, and ATMs in Jerusalem, providing a comprehensive overview of the services available.

Currency Options:

The official currency of Israel, including Jerusalem, is the Israeli New Shekel (ILS). It is denoted by the symbol "₪" or "ILS" and is subdivided into 100 agorot. The shekel comes in various denominations, including banknotes (20, 50, 100, and 200 shekels) and coins (1, 2, 5, and 10 shekels, as well as 10 and 50 agorot).

Accepted Currencies:

While the Israeli New Shekel is the primary currency accepted throughout Jerusalem, major international currencies such as the US Dollar (USD), Euro (EUR), and British Pound (GBP) are also commonly accepted at many hotels, restaurants, and larger establishments. However, it's advisable to carry local currency for smaller businesses, street vendors, and public transportation.

Banking System:

Jerusalem boasts a robust banking system, with numerous local and international banks operating branches throughout the city. Some of the prominent Israeli banks include Bank Hapoalim, Bank Leumi, Israel Discount Bank, and Mizrahi-Tefahot Bank. These banks provide a wide array of financial services, including currency exchange, money transfers, savings and checking accounts, loans, and investment opportunities.

Opening a Bank Account:

Both residents and non-residents can open bank accounts in Jerusalem. To open an account, individuals typically need to provide identification documents, proof of residence (for residents), and a minimum deposit. Non-residents may be required to present additional documentation, such as a passport and proof of income. It's recommended to contact the bank of choice in advance to confirm the requirements and schedule an appointment.

ATMs:

ATMs are widely available in Jerusalem, ensuring convenient access to cash. Most ATMs accept major credit and debit cards, including Visa, Mastercard, and American Express. In addition to Hebrew, many ATMs also offer language options, such as English and Arabic. It's advisable to inform your bank about your travel plans to ensure smooth access to funds and avoid any potential card blocks.

ATM Locations:

ATMs can be found throughout Jerusalem, including in banks, shopping centers, commercial areas, and tourist hubs. Commonly visited locations, such as the Old City, Mahane Yehuda Market, and Ben Yehuda Street, have several ATMs conveniently located. Additionally, many hotels and tourist information centers offer ATM services.

Currency Exchange:

Currency exchange services are readily available in Jerusalem. Banks, currency exchange offices, and authorized exchange booths (known as "Forex" or "Change" offices) offer currency conversion services. It's advisable to compare exchange rates and service fees before conducting any transactions to ensure you receive the best value for your money.

Safety and Security:

While Jerusalem, like any other major city, requires caution when handling financial matters, the banking and ATM systems in the city are generally safe and reliable. It is recommended to use ATMs located in well-lit and populated areas and be vigilant against any suspicious activity.

Jerusalem provides a robust banking infrastructure, a variety of currency options, and an extensive network of ATMs, ensuring convenience and accessibility for residents and visitors alike. By familiarizing yourself with the local currency, banking services, and ATM locations, you can navigate the financial landscape of Jerusalem with ease. Remember to exercise caution and prioritize personal safety when conducting financial transactions.

SAFETY TIPS AND EMERGENCY CONTACTS

Like any major city, it is important for residents and visitors to prioritize safety and be prepared for emergencies. This note provides valuable safety tips and emergency contact information to ensure a secure experience while exploring Jerusalem.

Safety Tips:

Stay Informed: Keep yourself updated on current events, travel advisories, and any security alerts issued by the local authorities or your embassy. Stay connected to reliable news sources and follow their guidance regarding safety precautions.

Respect Cultural Norms: Jerusalem is a city of diverse religious and cultural backgrounds. Show respect for local customs and traditions. Dress modestly when visiting religious sites, and be mindful of your behavior to avoid unintentionally offending anyone.

Be Aware of Your Surroundings: Pay attention to your surroundings and stay alert at all times. Avoid poorly lit or deserted areas, especially at night. Stick to well-populated and well-lit streets and use well-known and reliable transportation options.

Secure Your Belongings: Protect your valuables by keeping them secure and out of sight. Avoid displaying expensive items, such as jewelry or large amounts of cash. Use a concealed money belt or a secure bag to carry your belongings.

Use Reliable Transportation: When using public transportation or taxis, choose licensed and reputable providers. Avoid accepting rides from unmarked vehicles or strangers. If you're using ride-hailing services, ensure that the vehicle and driver match the details provided on the app.

Stay Connected: Share your itinerary and contact information with a trusted friend or family member. Keep a charged mobile phone with emergency numbers saved in your contacts. Consider using a local SIM card for better communication.

Emergency Preparedness: Familiarize yourself with emergency exits and evacuation plans of your accommodation, as well as key landmarks and evacuation routes in the city. Make sure you know the location of the nearest hospital, police station, and embassy.

Emergency Contacts:

Police: Dial 100 (or 911) for emergencies requiring immediate police assistance.

Ambulance: Dial 101 for medical emergencies or to request an ambulance.

Fire Department: Dial 102 in case of fire or any related emergency.

Tourist Police Hotline: +972-2-543-0339 (available 24/7) for non-emergency assistance, reporting incidents, or seeking information regarding safety concerns.

Embassy or Consulate: Contact your country's embassy or consulate in Jerusalem for assistance, including emergency situations and lost or stolen passports.

Jerusalem is a captivating city with a rich history, but it's important to prioritize safety during your visit. By following these safety tips, staying informed, and being prepared, you can enhance your overall experience and ensure a secure stay in Jerusalem. Remember to keep emergency contact numbers readily accessible and stay vigilant throughout your time in the city. Enjoy your time exploring the remarkable cultural and historical sites Jerusalem has to offer while maintaining a safe and secure environment.

LANGUAGE AND USEFUL PHRASES

Language plays a significant role in the cultural and historical fabric of Jerusalem, one of the oldest and most diverse cities in the world. As the capital of Israel, Jerusalem has a rich linguistic heritage shaped by various influences, including Hebrew, Arabic, English, and other languages spoken by the city's diverse population.

Hebrew and Arabic are the official languages of Jerusalem, reflecting the two major religious and cultural communities in the city: Jews and Arabs. Hebrew is the primary language spoken by the Jewish population, while Arabic is predominantly spoken by the Palestinian Arab population. Both languages carry immense cultural and religious significance, and knowing a few key phrases can greatly enhance your experience in Jerusalem.

Here are some useful phrases in both Hebrew and Arabic:

Hebrew:

Shalom (שָׁלוֹם) - Hello/Peace.

Todah (תּוֹדָה) - Thank you.

Boker tov (בּוֹקֶר טוֹב) - Good morning.

Erev tov (עֶרֶב טוֹב) - Good evening.

Slicha (סְלִיחָה) - Excuse me/Sorry.

Ani medaber/medaberet ivrit? (אֲנִי מְדַבֵּר/מְדַבֶּרֶת עִבְרִית) - Do you speak Hebrew? (masculine/feminine)

Eifo...? (אֵיפֹה) - Where is...?

Ani rotse/rotsa (masculine/feminine) la chatzot (לַחֲצוֹת) - I want to buy.

Arabic:

Marhaba (مَرْحَبًا) - Hello.

Shukran (شُكْرًا) - Thank you.

Sabah al-khair (صَبَاح الخَيْر) - Good morning.

Masa' al-khair (مَسَاء الخَيْر) - Good evening.

Afwan (عَفْوًا) - Excuse me/Sorry.

Hal tatakallam al-'arabiya? (هَلْ تَتَكَلَّم العَرَبِيَّة) - Do you speak Arabic?

Ain...? (أَيْنَ) - Where is...?

Biddi (بِدِّي) - I want.

English is widely understood and spoken in many parts of Jerusalem, particularly in tourist areas and among the younger generation. However, it's always a good idea to learn a few basic phrases in the local languages as a sign of respect and to facilitate communication, especially when interacting with older individuals or those who may not speak English fluently.

Moreover, Jerusalem is home to a diverse range of religious communities, each with its own distinct languages and dialects. For example, various Christian communities in the city may use languages such as Greek, Latin, Armenian, or other liturgical languages during religious services and ceremonies.

As a multicultural city, Jerusalem celebrates its linguistic diversity, and locals appreciate visitors who make an effort to engage with their languages and cultures. Whether you're exploring the Old City's historic sites, bargaining in the bustling markets, or engaging in conversations with locals, knowing a few phrases in Hebrew and Arabic can open doors to meaningful interactions and enrich your experience in this remarkable city.

CUSTOMS AND ETIQUETTE

Customs and etiquette play a vital role in Jerusalem, a city known for its rich historical and religious significance. As a place that is deeply revered by various faiths, including Judaism, Christianity, and

Islam, Jerusalem carries with it a unique set of cultural practices and expectations. Whether you are a visitor or a resident, it is important to be mindful of these customs and etiquette to show respect and foster harmonious interactions. Here is a comprehensive guide to customs and etiquette in Jerusalem:

Dress modestly: Jerusalem is a conservative city, particularly in its religious neighborhoods. When visiting religious sites such as the Western Wall, the Church of the Holy Sepulchre, or the Al-Aqsa Mosque, both men and women should dress modestly. This means covering your shoulders, avoiding revealing clothing, and wearing long pants or skirts that cover the knees.

Respect religious sites: Jerusalem is home to numerous religious sites that are of utmost importance to different faiths. When visiting these sites, be respectful of the religious practices and rules. Dress appropriately, remove your shoes when required, and refrain from taking photographs or engaging in loud conversations unless it is permitted.

Greeting customs: The traditional greeting in Jerusalem is "Shalom" (in Hebrew) or "Salaam" (in Arabic), both of which mean "peace." When meeting someone, it is polite to offer a warm handshake, and in more formal settings, a slight bow may be appropriate. Men should avoid initiating physical contact with women unless they extend their hand first.

Sabbath observance: The Sabbath, which begins at sunset on Friday and ends at sunset on Saturday, is a significant time for observant Jews in Jerusalem. During this period, many shops and businesses may close, and public transportation may be limited. It is important to respect the religious practices of the city's Jewish population during the Sabbath by refraining from loud activities, photography, or non-essential work.

Kosher and Halal practices: Jerusalem has a diverse population that includes observant Jews and Muslims. It is important to be mindful of dietary restrictions when interacting with locals or dining out. Kosher food follows Jewish dietary laws, while Halal food adheres to Islamic dietary guidelines. Respect these practices by avoiding the consumption of pork or mixing meat and dairy products when sharing a meal with observant individuals.

Tipping: Tipping in Jerusalem is customary and is generally around 10-15% of the bill in restaurants and cafes. Some establishments may include a service charge, so it's worth checking the bill before tipping. It is also customary to tip hotel staff, tour guides, and taxi drivers, although the amount may vary depending on the quality of service.

Language: Jerusalem is a multilingual city, with Hebrew, Arabic, and English being the most commonly spoken languages. While English is widely understood, it is respectful to learn a few basic phrases in Hebrew or Arabic to communicate with locals. Simple greetings and expressions of gratitude can go a long way in creating positive interactions.

Be mindful of religious sensitivities: Jerusalem is a city where religious sensitivities run deep. Avoid engaging in conversations or actions that may be disrespectful or offensive to any particular faith. Be mindful of your surroundings, particularly in religiously significant areas, and follow any instructions or guidelines provided by authorities or religious leaders.

Photography and privacy: Jerusalem is a city with countless picturesque sites, but it's important to be respectful when taking photographs. Always ask for permission before photographing individuals, especially in religious neighborhoods. Respect any signs or instructions regarding photography restrictions in certain areas, as some religious sites prohibit photography altogether.

Punctuality and patience: It is customary to be punctual for appointments and meetings in Jerusalem. However, it is also important to have patience and flexibility, as cultural practices and religious events may occasionally cause delays or changes in plans. Demonstrating understanding and adaptability will help create a positive experience for everyone involved.

By adhering to these customs and etiquette, you can navigate Jerusalem with respect and sensitivity, creating meaningful connections and fostering a greater appreciation for the city's diverse religious and cultural heritage. Remember, Jerusalem is a place where people from different backgrounds converge, and by embracing its customs, you contribute to the spirit of unity and coexistence that defines this remarkable city.

CHAPTER SIX: DAY TRIPS FROM JERUSALEM:

BETHLEHEM AND THE CHURCH OF THE NATIVITY

A popular day trip from Jerusalem is to visit Bethlehem and the Church of the Nativity. Bethlehem is an important biblical site and is located just a few kilometers south of Jerusalem in the West Bank. Here's some information about visiting Bethlehem and the Church of the Nativity:

Getting There: From Jerusalem, you can take a local bus, a guided tour, or a taxi to Bethlehem. The journey usually takes around 30 minutes, depending on traffic and the checkpoint crossing. Make sure to check the current travel regulations and security situation before planning your visit, as conditions may vary.

Church of the Nativity: The Church of the Nativity is one of the oldest surviving Christian churches in the world. It is believed to be built on the site where Jesus Christ was born. The church complex includes the Grotto of the Nativity, which marks the exact spot of the birthplace, as well as the Church of St. Catherine and the Church of St. Joseph.

Manger Square: Located in front of the Church of the Nativity, Manger Square is a bustling square and a focal point of Bethlehem. It is lined with shops, cafes, and restaurants, and it's a great place to soak up the local atmosphere.

Shepherds' Field: Another significant site in Bethlehem is the Shepherds' Field, which is located a short distance from the Church of the Nativity. It is believed to be the place where the shepherds were visited by angels and informed about the birth of Jesus. There are several churches and monasteries in the area, including the Franciscan Chapel and the Greek Orthodox Church of the Shepherds.

Palestinian Culture and Handicrafts: Bethlehem offers an opportunity to explore Palestinian culture and traditions. You can visit local handicraft shops and cooperatives to purchase traditional olive wood carvings, ceramics, and embroidery. Additionally, you may get a chance to try delicious Palestinian cuisine at the local restaurants.

It's worth noting that visiting Bethlehem requires passing through a security checkpoint due to its location in the West Bank. Therefore, it's advisable to check the current situation and any travel advisories before planning your day trip.

Remember to carry your passport and any necessary identification documents, as they may be required at the checkpoint.

MASADA AND THE DEAD SEA

Jerusalem, a city rich in history and spirituality, offers a multitude of fascinating sights and experiences. While exploring this ancient city, it is worth taking a day trip to visit two incredible destinations nearby: Masada and the Dead Sea. These iconic sites provide a unique opportunity to delve into Israel's past and indulge in the natural wonders of the region.

Masada, located on a rocky plateau overlooking the Dead Sea, holds immense historical significance. The story of Masada is one of heroism and resilience, making it a must-visit site for history enthusiasts. The fortress was built by King Herod the Great and served as a palace complex. However, its most memorable chapter unfolded during the Jewish revolt against the Romans in the first century AD.

After Jerusalem fell to the Romans in 70 AD, a group of Jewish rebels, known as the Zealots, sought refuge at Masada. The Romans laid siege to the fortress, but the rebels held their ground for several years. Eventually, realizing defeat was inevitable, the Zealots made a tragic decision. Rather than falling into the hands of their enemies, they chose mass suicide. This act of defiance became a symbol of Jewish resistance and national pride.

Visiting Masada today is a powerful experience. Ascending the plateau can be done via a cable car or by climbing the

Snake Path, a steep trail offering stunning views along the way. Upon reaching the summit, visitors can explore the well-preserved ruins of the palace complex, including Herod's luxurious palace, Roman bathhouses, and storerooms. The most moving part of the visit is witnessing the remains of the fortifications and the poignant story of the Zealots etched into the stones.

After immersing yourself in the historical wonders of Masada, the journey continues to the nearby Dead Sea. Known as the lowest point on Earth, the Dead Sea is a natural marvel and a unique destination for travelers. The sea's saline water and mineral-rich mud have attracted visitors for centuries, offering healing properties and a truly unforgettable experience.

As you approach the Dead Sea, you'll notice its striking beauty. The waters shimmer with a mesmerizing turquoise hue, surrounded by desert landscapes and rugged mountains. The high salt concentration of the sea makes it impossible for any living creature, except for certain types of bacteria, to survive in its waters. This extreme salinity allows visitors to effortlessly float on the surface, creating a sensation of weightlessness that is both relaxing and amusing.

Taking a dip in the Dead Sea is a one-of-a-kind experience. As you lie back and let the buoyant water support your body, you can feel the healing properties of the minerals seep into your skin. The Dead Sea mud, renowned for its therapeutic qualities, is also readily available along the shores. Smearing this mineral-rich mud on your skin is believed to improve various skin conditions, leaving it feeling rejuvenated and refreshed.

Apart from floating and indulging in the mud, the Dead Sea region offers additional attractions. There are several luxury resorts and spas that provide an array of treatments, ranging from massages to salt scrubs, all utilizing the sea's natural resources. Moreover, the surrounding landscapes are perfect for hiking and exploring the desert scenery, providing a contrasting experience to the historical sites in Jerusalem.

When planning a day trip from Jerusalem to Masada and the Dead Sea, it is advisable to allocate ample time for both destinations. While Masada can be explored in a few hours, the Dead Sea invites you to relax and take in its wonders. Remember to bring a hat, sunscreen, and plenty of water, as the desert climate can be intense. Additionally, it is worth noting that both sites are significant in Israeli history, and paying respect to their cultural and religious importance is essential.

In conclusion, a day trip from Jerusalem to Masada and the Dead Sea is a remarkable journey through history and nature. From the awe-inspiring ruins of Masada to the rejuvenating experience of floating in the Dead Sea, these destinations offer an unforgettable combination of historical exploration and natural relaxation. Whether you're a history enthusiast, a nature lover, or simply seeking a unique experience, this day trip promises to be an enriching adventure in the heart of Israel.

EIN GEDI NATURE RESERVE

Ein Gedi Nature Reserve is a remarkable destination for day trips from Jerusalem. Located on the eastern shore of the Dead Sea, this breathtaking oasis offers a unique blend of natural beauty, fascinating history, and abundant wildlife. Whether you're a nature enthusiast, a history buff, or simply seeking a peaceful retreat, Ein Gedi has something to offer everyone.

The journey from Jerusalem to Ein Gedi is relatively short, taking approximately 45 minutes to an hour by car. As you leave the bustling city behind, you'll be greeted by the stark desert landscape, which only serves to enhance the allure of Ein Gedi's lush greenery and cascading waterfalls.

Upon arrival at the nature reserve, you'll find yourself surrounded by an oasis teeming with life. Ein Gedi boasts an astonishing variety of plant species, many of which are unique to this region. The sight of vibrant palm trees, wildflowers, and thickets of acacia and tamarisk creates a stark contrast against the arid backdrop.

One of the highlights of Ein Gedi is its series of freshwater springs and waterfalls. The most famous of these is the David Waterfall, named after King David who sought refuge in this very area while fleeing from King Saul. The sight of water tumbling down rocky cliffs into crystal-clear pools is truly mesmerizing. Visitors have the opportunity to take refreshing dips in the pools, offering respite from the desert heat.

For those who enjoy hiking, Ein Gedi offers several well-marked trails of varying difficulty levels. The Wadi David trail is particularly popular, leading you along the course of the stream, past the David Waterfall, and up to a higher waterfall known as the Shulamit Waterfall. The hike is relatively easy and provides ample opportunities to spot wildlife such as ibexes, rock hyraxes, and numerous bird species.

Another noteworthy attraction within Ein Gedi is the Ein Gedi Botanical Garden. This meticulously maintained garden showcases a vast array of plant species from around the world, including cacti, succulents, and medicinal plants. Strolling through the garden's pathways, you'll be enchanted by the vibrant colors, intoxicating fragrances, and the serene atmosphere.

For history enthusiasts, Ein Gedi also holds archaeological significance. The remains of an ancient synagogue dating back to the 3rd century CE can be explored, offering a glimpse into the region's rich Jewish heritage. The synagogue's mosaic floors, adorned with intricate geometric patterns and biblical motifs, are truly remarkable.

In addition to its natural and historical attractions, Ein Gedi offers various amenities to enhance visitors' experiences. The nature reserve features picnic areas equipped with tables and shaded gazebos, providing the perfect setting for a relaxing outdoor meal. There is also a visitor center where you can learn more about the reserve's flora, fauna, and history through informative displays and interactive exhibits.

Overall, a day trip to Ein Gedi Nature Reserve from Jerusalem promises a memorable experience filled with awe-inspiring landscapes, refreshing waterfalls, diverse wildlife, and intriguing history. Whether you're seeking adventure, tranquility, or a deeper connection with nature, this oasis in the desert will captivate your senses and leave you with lasting memories of Israel's natural wonders.

QUMRAN AND THE DEAD SEA SCROLLS

If you find yourself in Jerusalem and are looking for an enriching day trip that combines history, spirituality, and natural wonders, a visit to Qumran and the Dead Sea Scrolls is highly recommended. This excursion will take you back in time to one of the most significant archaeological discoveries of the 20th century and allow you to experience the unique beauty of the Dead Sea region.

Qumran, located approximately 25 kilometers east of Jerusalem, is an archaeological site that gained worldwide recognition due to the discovery of the Dead Sea Scrolls in the mid-20th century. These ancient manuscripts, which include some of the earliest known copies of biblical texts, shed light on the religious and historical context of the Second Temple period. Exploring the site provides a fascinating glimpse into the lives of the Jewish sect that inhabited Qumran around 2,000 years ago.

To begin your day trip, you can either rent a car or join a guided tour from Jerusalem. The journey to Qumran takes around one hour, and along the way, you'll witness the dramatic change in landscape as you descend from the hills surrounding

Jerusalem to the lowest point on Earth, where the Dead Sea is located.

Once you arrive at Qumran, you'll be greeted by a visitor center that offers an informative introduction to the history and significance of the Dead Sea Scrolls. Knowledgeable guides and multimedia exhibits provide valuable context, allowing you to appreciate the importance of this archaeological treasure. The exhibition includes replicas of the caves where the scrolls were found, giving you a sense of the environment in which they were hidden for centuries.

After immersing yourself in the story of the Dead Sea Scrolls, you can explore the actual archaeological site. The ruins of Qumran consist of various structures, including a communal dining hall, living quarters, a scriptorium, and a ritual bath, or mikveh. These remnants provide insight into the unique lifestyle and practices of the Essene community, the religious sect believed to have authored the scrolls.

As you stroll through the ruins, you can visualize the ancient inhabitants going about their daily lives, engaging in religious rituals, and studying and transcribing sacred texts. The landscape surrounding Qumran is also breathtaking, with the rugged cliffs and the Dead Sea forming a stunning backdrop.

After your visit to Qumran, you can continue your day trip by heading to one of the beaches along the Dead Sea. The Dead Sea, famous for its high salt content, allows you to experience the surreal sensation of effortlessly floating on its buoyant waters. You can relax and enjoy the therapeutic benefits of the mineral-rich mud, which is believed to have healing properties for the skin.

While swimming in the Dead Sea, you can marvel at the unique landscapes surrounding you. The stark beauty of the salt-encrusted shores, the barren mountains, and the hazy horizon create an otherworldly atmosphere that is truly unforgettable. The Dead Sea region is also home to various resorts and spas where you can pamper yourself with rejuvenating treatments and massages.

Before you leave the area, be sure to catch a magnificent sunset over the Dead Sea. As the sun sinks below the horizon, it casts a golden glow on the water, creating a spectacle of colors that will leave you in awe.

A day trip from Jerusalem to Qumran and the Dead Sea Scrolls offers a blend of history, spirituality, and natural wonders. It allows you to delve into the mysteries of the past, gain a deeper understanding of ancient Jewish culture, and experience the unparalleled beauty of the Dead Sea region. Whether you're a history enthusiast, a nature lover, or simply seeking a unique and enriching experience, this excursion is bound to leave a lasting impression.

JERICHO

Jericho, located in the West Bank, is a fascinating destination for a day trip from Jerusalem. Known as the "City of Palms," it holds immense historical and biblical significance, making it an ideal place to explore for those interested in archaeology, religion, and ancient civilizations. In this note, I will delve into the various attractions and experiences that Jericho offers to visitors.

One of the most iconic landmarks in Jericho is the ancient city of Jericho itself. Considered to be one of the oldest inhabited cities in the world, Jericho boasts a rich history dating back thousands of years. Its archaeological sites offer a glimpse into the city's ancient past, allowing visitors to witness the remnants of ancient civilizations that once thrived there. The most notable archaeological site in Jericho is Tell es-Sultan, which includes the remains of the walls and towers of the ancient city, as well as the famous Jericho Tower, dating back to the Neolithic period.

Another must-visit attraction in Jericho is the Monastery of the Temptation. Located on a cliff overlooking the city, this Greek Orthodox monastery holds great significance in Christian tradition. It is believed to be the site where Jesus was tempted by the devil during his 40-day fast in the wilderness. Visitors can reach the monastery by cable car or by hiking up the path that winds through the mountainous terrain, providing stunning views along the way.

Nature enthusiasts will also find plenty to appreciate in Jericho. The city is blessed with a unique geographical setting, surrounded by stunning landscapes that offer opportunities for outdoor adventures. The nearby Mount of Temptation, apart from hosting the monastery, is a popular spot for hiking and rock climbing. The area also features lush palm groves and natural springs, creating a serene oasis amidst the arid desert landscape.

For those seeking a more leisurely experience, a visit to the Dead Sea is highly recommended. Located just a short distance from Jericho, the Dead Sea is the lowest point on Earth and famous for its high salt concentration, allowing visitors to effortlessly float on its surface. Besides enjoying the buoyancy of the water, one can indulge in the therapeutic benefits of the Dead Sea mud, renowned for its rejuvenating properties.

Furthermore, Jericho's proximity to the Jordan River makes it an excellent base for exploring biblical sites. Qasr al-Yahud, located on the banks of the river, is believed to be the site of Jesus' baptism. Pilgrims from all over the world visit this sacred spot, and some even participate in baptismal rituals themselves. The serene and spiritual atmosphere of the area makes it a profoundly meaningful experience for many visitors.

In terms of local cuisine, Jericho offers a delectable array of traditional Palestinian dishes. From mouthwatering falafels and hummus to sumptuous grilled meats and fresh salads, the local culinary scene is sure to delight food enthusiasts. Exploring the bustling markets and tasting the authentic flavors of Jericho is an experience not to be missed.

In conclusion, a day trip from Jerusalem to Jericho is a journey through time and spirituality. The city's archaeological sites, religious landmarks, natural beauty, and culinary delights combine to create a truly unforgettable experience. Whether you're interested in history, religion, outdoor activities, or simply seeking a unique cultural immersion, Jericho has something to offer every visitor.

YAD KENNEDY AND THE JERUSALEM HILLS

Yad Kennedy, also known as the John F. Kennedy Memorial, is situated in the beautiful Jerusalem Forest, just a short drive away from the city. This memorial was built in honor of the late President John F. Kennedy, who had a profound impact on the relationship between the United States and Israel. The memorial's location was chosen for its scenic beauty and tranquility, providing visitors with a serene setting for reflection and remembrance.

As you arrive at Yad Kennedy, you will be greeted by a striking 60-foot high stone monument, resembling a truncated cone. The design symbolizes an ancient Roman tower and serves as a tribute to Kennedy's admiration for classical antiquity. The monument stands on a hilltop, offering panoramic views of the surrounding countryside, including the stunning Jerusalem Hills.

The Jerusalem Hills, extending to the west of Jerusalem, are a picturesque region characterized by rolling hills, verdant landscapes, and charming villages. Exploring this area is a delightful way to escape the bustling city and immerse yourself in the natural beauty of the Israeli countryside.

One popular activity in the Jerusalem Hills is hiking. There are numerous well-marked trails that cater to various skill levels, allowing visitors to choose their preferred level of difficulty. As you traverse the hills, you'll encounter ancient ruins, terraced vineyards, and olive groves, all steeped in history and cultural significance.

One of the notable trails in the region is the Burma Road Trail. This historic route served as a crucial supply route during the 1948 Arab-Israeli War. Following this trail will take you through scenic landscapes and offer glimpses into the past. Another renowned trail is the Israel National Trail, which stretches from the northernmost point of Israel to its southernmost tip, offering hikers an incredible journey through diverse landscapes.

Apart from hiking, the Jerusalem Hills are also home to several charming villages and cultural sites worth exploring. Ein Karem, for example, is a picturesque village nestled in the hills, known for its tranquil atmosphere, quaint stone houses, and religious significance. It is believed to be the birthplace of John the Baptist and has numerous churches and monasteries that attract pilgrims from around the world.

Another village worth visiting is Abu Ghosh, renowned for its beautiful church, the Church of the Resurrection of the Crusader era. This village is also famous for its delectable Middle Eastern cuisine, particularly its hummus, attracting food enthusiasts and travelers alike.

In conclusion, taking a day trip from Jerusalem to visit Yad Kennedy and explore the Jerusalem Hills is a captivating and enriching experience. Yad Kennedy provides an opportunity for reflection and pays homage to a prominent historical figure, while the Jerusalem Hills offer a tranquil escape into nature, with scenic hikes, picturesque villages, and cultural sites to discover. These day trips allow visitors to appreciate the diversity and beauty of Israel beyond the ancient walls of Jerusalem and create lasting memories of their journey.

CHAPTER SEVEN: DINING AND CULINARY EXPERIENCE

TRADITIONAL ISRAELI CUISINE AND LOCAL DELICACIES

Traditional Israeli cuisine is a vibrant and diverse culinary tapestry that reflects the country's rich history, cultural influences, and geographical location. Israel's culinary traditions draw from the culinary practices of Jewish diaspora communities, Middle Eastern flavors, Mediterranean ingredients, and the incorporation of local produce. The result is a unique fusion of flavors, textures, and cooking techniques that make Israeli cuisine a delight for food enthusiasts.

One of the hallmarks of Israeli cuisine is the emphasis on fresh and seasonal ingredients. The country's favorable climate allows for the cultivation of a wide variety of fruits, vegetables, and herbs, which form the backbone of many dishes. Some of the prominent ingredients in Israeli cuisine include olives, citrus fruits, pomegranates, tomatoes, cucumbers, eggplants, and a myriad of fresh herbs like parsley, mint, and cilantro.

One of the most famous dishes in Israeli cuisine is falafel. These deep-fried balls or patties made from ground chickpeas or fava beans are often served in pita bread with a variety of toppings such as tahini sauce, hummus, pickles, and salad. Falafel is a beloved street food that can be found in every corner of the country and has gained popularity worldwide.

Hummus is another staple of Israeli cuisine. Made from mashed chickpeas, tahini (sesame seed paste), lemon juice, garlic, and olive oil, hummus is a versatile and creamy dip that is often served as an appetizer or as a condiment with various dishes. It is typically enjoyed with fresh pita bread or as a component of a mezze platter.

Shawarma is a beloved street food in Israel and a favorite among locals and tourists alike. It consists of marinated slices of meat, traditionally lamb or chicken, which are roasted on a vertical spit. The meat is then thinly sliced and served in a pita or laffa bread with various toppings such as tahini, salad, pickles, and amba, a tangy mango sauce. Shawarma is a flavorful and satisfying meal that perfectly encapsulates the fusion of Middle Eastern and Israeli culinary influences.

Sabich is another popular Israeli street food that originated from the Iraqi Jewish community. It consists of a warm pita bread filled with fried eggplant slices, hard-boiled eggs, Israeli salad (chopped tomatoes and cucumbers), tahini sauce, and amba. Sabich is a delicious and hearty sandwich that showcases the diverse flavors and textures found in Israeli cuisine.

In addition to these well-known dishes, Israeli cuisine boasts a wide array of local delicacies and regional specialties. For instance, Jerusalem is renowned for its slow-cooked meat dishes such as lamb shoulder or beef in a rich tomato and vegetable sauce. The coastal city of Jaffa is famous for its fresh seafood, particularly grilled or fried fish, served with a squeeze of lemon and a side of tahini sauce.

The Galilee region in northern Israel is known for its culinary traditions influenced by the local Arab communities. Mansaf, a traditional Bedouin dish, is a prime example. It consists of tender lamb cooked in a fermented yogurt sauce, served over a bed of rice and garnished with almonds and parsley. This dish is often enjoyed during festive occasions and special gatherings.

Desserts hold a special place in Israeli cuisine, with sweet treats like baklava, halva, and rugelach gracing many tables. Rugelach, in particular, is a Jewish pastry that consists of a cream cheese-based dough filled with various ingredients such as chocolate, nuts, and fruit preserves. It is rolled into a crescent shape and baked until golden and flaky.

Moreover, Israel's wine industry has gained international recognition in recent years, with a growing number of wineries producing high-quality wines. The country's diverse terroir and Mediterranean climate provide ideal conditions for cultivating grapes, resulting in a range of wines that are both robust and elegant.

In conclusion, traditional Israeli cuisine is a celebration of flavors, aromas, and cultural influences. From the vibrant street food scene to the rich and diverse regional dishes, Israeli cuisine offers a culinary adventure that is sure to please any palate. Whether indulging in the beloved falafel, savoring the creamy hummus, or enjoying the diverse range of local delicacies, exploring Israeli cuisine is a journey that will leave you with a deep appreciation for the country's culinary heritage.

RESTAURANTS AND CAFES FOR VARIOUS BUDGETS

The city of Jerusalem offers a wide range of restaurants and cafes catering to various budgets. Whether you're looking for an upscale dining experience or a quick bite on a budget, Jerusalem has something to offer for every taste and wallet. Let's explore some of the top restaurants and cafes in Jerusalem for different budgets.

High-End Dining:

a. Machneyuda: Located in the vibrant Mahane Yehuda market, Machneyuda offers a unique dining experience with its modern Israeli cuisine. The menu is inspired by local ingredients, and the lively atmosphere adds to the overall charm of the place.

b. Mona: Situated in the heart of the city, Mona is a Michelin-starred restaurant that specializes in contemporary Mediterranean cuisine. The elegant setting, exceptional service, and innovative dishes make it an ideal choice for a special occasion.

Mid-Range Options:

a. Azura: Known for its delicious home-cooked style Middle Eastern food, Azura is a popular spot in the Old City. The restaurant has been serving its signature dishes, including hummus, falafel, and stuffed vegetables, for decades, attracting locals and tourists alike.

b. Café Hillel: Located in the German Colony neighborhood, Café Hillel is a casual eatery offering a diverse menu of sandwiches, salads, and pastas. It's a great place to grab a quick and satisfying meal without breaking the bank.

Budget-Friendly Eateries:

a. Marzipan Bakery: This bakery, situated in the heart of the Jewish Quarter, is famous for its mouthwatering rugelach and pastries. It's an excellent option for a budget-friendly breakfast or afternoon snack while exploring the surrounding historic sites.

b. Hummus Ben Sira: As the name suggests, this small hummus joint on Ben Sira Street serves some of the best hummus in the city. The prices are affordable, and the portions are generous, making it a go-to spot for hummus enthusiasts.

Vegetarian and Vegan:

a. Tala Hummus and Falafel: This vegetarian and vegan-friendly restaurant in the Mahane Yehuda market offers a variety of delicious falafel, hummus, and freshly prepared salads. The friendly staff and affordable prices make it a popular choice among locals and visitors.

b. Nafoura: Situated near the Damascus Gate, Nafoura specializes in Middle Eastern vegetarian and vegan dishes. The menu includes options like stuffed grape leaves, moussaka, and falafel, ensuring a satisfying dining experience for plant-based food lovers.

Coffee Shops and Cafes:

a. Aroma Espresso Bar: With multiple branches across the city, Aroma is a well-known Israeli coffee chain. They serve a range of coffee beverages, sandwiches, and pastries, making it an ideal spot for a quick caffeine fix or a light meal.

b. Roladin: This popular bakery chain offers a variety of pastries, cakes, and sandwiches, along with a selection of hot and cold drinks. It's a great place to relax and enjoy a cup of coffee while indulging in some sweet treats.

Remember, these are just a few examples of the diverse dining options available in Jerusalem. The city's culinary scene is ever-evolving, with new restaurants and cafes constantly opening up. Whether you're a food enthusiast or simply looking to enjoy a delicious meal, Jerusalem has a plethora of choices to suit every budget and palate.

KOSHER FOOD OPTIONS AND RECOMMENDATIONS

The capital city of Israel, holds a special place in the hearts of many due to its rich history, cultural significance, and religious importance. As a result, Jerusalem offers a wide array of kosher food options for locals and visitors alike. This note aims to provide an overview of the kosher food scene in Jerusalem, highlighting some popular venues, recommendations, and guidelines for those seeking kosher dining experiences.

Understanding Kosher:

Kosher refers to food that adheres to Jewish dietary laws and regulations outlined in the Torah. Observing kosher practices involves specific rules regarding the types of animals that can be consumed, how animals are slaughtered, separation of dairy and meat products, and the certification of ingredients and food preparation processes.

Kosher Certification:

In Jerusalem, kosher food establishments are required to obtain certification from recognized kosher authorities. The most common kosher certifications you will encounter are the "kosher" symbol (a "K" inside a circle) or the word "kosher" in Hebrew letters. These symbols signify that the establishment adheres to the strict guidelines of kosher food preparation.

Kosher Food Options:

Kosher Restaurants: Jerusalem boasts an impressive selection of kosher restaurants, ranging from traditional Jewish cuisine to modern fusion dishes. Some renowned kosher restaurants include Machneyuda, a trendy and vibrant eatery known for its innovative dishes, and Touro, which offers a fine dining experience with a focus on grilled meats. Other popular options include Angelica, Canela, and Chakra.

Kosher Cafes and Bakeries: Jerusalem is home to numerous kosher cafes and bakeries, perfect for a quick bite or a relaxing cup of coffee. Café Rimon, located in the heart of the city, offers a diverse menu featuring dairy and meat dishes. Marzipan Bakery is famous for its delectable pastries and fresh bread. For a charming atmosphere and delicious kosher treats, try Café Bezalel or Café Hillel.

Kosher Street Food: Exploring the streets of Jerusalem will reveal a plethora of kosher street food options that cater to diverse tastes. The Mahane Yehuda Market, commonly known as "The Shuk," is a vibrant hub for kosher street food vendors. You can find an assortment of delectable snacks like falafel, shawarma, sabich, and more. Be sure to try the renowned fried cheese balls at Azura or the mouthwatering malawach at Hatzot.

Kosher Recommendations:

Shabbat Experience: Experience an authentic Shabbat (Sabbath) meal by booking a Friday night dinner at one of the kosher restaurants in Jerusalem. These dinners typically offer traditional Jewish dishes such as challah bread, gefilte fish, matzo ball soup, and slow-cooked meats. The joyful ambiance and communal nature of Shabbat meals make for a truly memorable experience.

Kosher Markets: Visit the Mahane Yehuda Market, where you can immerse yourself in the vibrant atmosphere while exploring a wide variety of fresh produce, spices, kosher meats, and other culinary delights. This is an excellent opportunity to sample local kosher ingredients and discover unique flavors.

Kosher Cooking Workshops: Several establishments in Jerusalem offer kosher cooking workshops where you can learn to prepare traditional Jewish dishes. These workshops provide an educational and hands-on experience, allowing you to explore the rich culinary heritage of Jerusalem.

Kosher Food Tours: Consider joining a kosher food tour to gain a deeper understanding of Jerusalem's kosher cuisine. These tours often include visits to various kosher eateries, historical sites, and expert-guided commentary on the significance of kosher food in Jewish culture.

Jerusalem offers a diverse range of kosher food options that cater to both traditional and contemporary pilates. From renowned kosher restaurants to charming cafes and bustling street food vendors, the city provides an abundance of culinary experiences rooted in Jewish traditions. Exploring Jerusalem's kosher food scene allows visitors to not only satisfy their taste buds but also gain a deeper appreciation for Jewish culture and cuisine.

Street food and food markets

Jerusalem, the captivating and culturally rich city, is not only a historical and religious hub but also a food lover's paradise. Its diverse culinary scene includes a plethora of street food stalls and bustling food markets that offer an array of flavors and aromas from different cultures and traditions. In this note, we will delve into the enticing world of street food and food markets in Jerusalem, where you can embark on a delightful gastronomic journey.

The Old City Markets:

The Old City of Jerusalem is a UNESCO World Heritage Site and home to some of the oldest and most vibrant markets in the world. The markets, known as "souks," are a maze of narrow, winding streets lined with colorful stalls and shops. Here, you can find an assortment of street food options and fresh produce, spices, sweets, and local delicacies.

Mahane Yehuda Market:

One of the most renowned food markets in Jerusalem is Mahane Yehuda. Located just outside the Old City walls, it is a bustling hub of activity and culinary delights. The market is a sensory overload, filled with the intoxicating aroma of spices, freshly baked bread, and a wide variety of local produce.

You can explore the stalls and indulge in mouth watering street food such as falafel, shawarma, sabich (a sandwich with fried eggplant and hard-boiled eggs), and a diverse range of Middle Eastern sweets. Don't miss trying the iconic Jerusalem bagel, which is crisp on the outside and soft on the inside.

Arab Shuk:

The Arab Shuk, also known as the Muslim Quarter, is located within the Old City. It offers a unique culinary experience with its vibrant street food stalls and traditional delicacies. Wander through the bustling alleys and savor dishes like musakhan (roasted chicken with sumac and caramelized onions on flatbread), kanafeh (a sweet cheese pastry soaked in syrup), and freshly squeezed pomegranate juice.

Armenian Quarter Market:

Situated in the Armenian Quarter of the Old City, this market is a hidden gem. The market is a treasure trove of Armenian delights, including homemade pastries, sweet and savory dishes, and unique spices. Be sure to try sujuk (spiced Armenian sausage), kadayif (shredded filo dough dessert), and indulge in the rich flavors of traditional Armenian coffee.

Street Food Hotspots:

Apart from the markets, Jerusalem boasts numerous street food hotspots where you can find delectable treats prepared right in front of you.

Abu Shukri:

This iconic establishment, located near the Damascus Gate, has been serving up delicious hummus and falafel for decades. The creamy hummus, drizzled with olive oil and sprinkled with paprika, pairs perfectly with their fluffy falafel and freshly baked pita bread.

Lina Falafel:

Located in the heart of downtown Jerusalem, Lina Falafel is a local favorite. Their falafel balls are crispy on the outside, tender on the inside, and bursting with flavor. Enjoy them stuffed in pita bread with an assortment of fresh vegetables and tahini sauce.

Zalatimo:

If you have a sweet tooth, make your way to Zalatimo, a family-owned pastry shop near the Church of the Holy Sepulchre. Their specialty is mutabbaq, a mouthwatering pastry filled with either sweet cheese or nuts. The delicate layers of pastry are baked to perfection, creating a delightful blend of textures.

Jerusalem's street food and food markets offer an extraordinary culinary experience that reflects the city's rich history and cultural diversity. From the vibrant markets of the Old City to the hidden street food gems scattered throughout the city, you'll find yourself immersed in a world of tantalizing flavors and aromas. So, when you visit Jerusalem, be sure to embark on a culinary adventure, exploring the bustling markets and indulging in the mouth watering street food that makes this city a true gastronomic haven.

CHAPTER EIGHT: SHOPPING

SOUVENIRS AND TRADITIONAL CRAFTS

Jerusalem is a treasure trove of cultural heritage and craftsmanship. It is home to a vibrant marketplace that offers an array of souvenirs and traditional crafts, each telling a unique story. From intricately designed ceramics to delicate hand-woven textiles, Jerusalem's artisanal creations reflect the city's diverse religious, historical, and cultural influences. In this note, we will delve into the world of Jerusalem's souvenirs and traditional crafts, showcasing their significance and the skills behind their creation.

Cultural Significance:

Jerusalem's souvenirs and traditional crafts hold great cultural significance, serving as tangible representations of the city's heritage. Visitors and locals alike can immerse themselves in the rich traditions and religious symbolism encapsulated within these art forms. Whether it's the olive wood carvings that pay homage to the biblical roots of the region or the intricate metalwork that showcases the city's historical Islamic influence, each souvenir serves as a tangible connection to Jerusalem's cultural fabric.

Handcrafted Ceramics:

Ceramics have been an integral part of Jerusalem's craftsmanship for centuries. From the iconic blue and white patterns of

Armenian pottery to the vibrant hues of Palestinian ceramics, the city's ceramic souvenirs display a range of techniques and motifs. The art of pottery-making involves shaping clay by hand, decorating it with intricate designs, and firing it in kilns. The result is a stunning collection of bowls, plates, tiles, and decorative items that capture the essence of Jerusalem's artistic heritage.

Embroidery and Textiles:
Embroidery is another traditional craft deeply rooted in Jerusalem's cultural identity. Palestinian and Israeli artisans skillfully create intricate patterns using various stitching techniques and vibrant threads. The motifs often draw inspiration from nature, geometric shapes, and

religious symbols. Traditional garments like the Palestinian thobe and the Jewish yarmulke are adorned with delicate embroidery, showcasing the artistry and craftsmanship passed down through generations.

Olive Wood Carvings:

Olive wood, abundant in the region, has been used for centuries to create unique and beautiful souvenirs. Skilled artisans hand-carve intricate designs into olive wood, producing items such as nativity scenes, crosses, chess sets, and decorative boxes. These carvings are not only aesthetically pleasing but also carry a deep spiritual meaning, as olive trees hold symbolic significance in various religious traditions, including Christianity and Judaism.

Metalwork and Jewelry:

Jerusalem's metalwork industry is renowned for its intricacy and attention to detail. The craft of metalwork encompasses techniques such as filigree, inlay, and repoussé. Skilled artisans create exquisite pieces of jewelry, including necklaces, bracelets, earrings, and rings, adorned with religious motifs, gemstones, and delicate patterns. The city's bustling markets are filled with shops that showcase these stunning metal creations, offering visitors a chance to take home a piece of Jerusalem's beauty.

Calligraphy and Illumination:

Calligraphy, the art of beautiful writing, is a cherished tradition in Jerusalem. Arabic and Hebrew calligraphy are particularly prominent, featuring prominently in religious texts, manuscripts, and decorative artwork. Skilled calligraphers meticulously craft intricate letters, words, and phrases, bringing to life the profound teachings and prayers of various religious traditions. Illuminated manuscripts, adorned with gold leaf and vibrant colors, exemplify the artistic mastery of Jerusalem's scribes.

Exploring Jerusalem's souvenirs and traditional crafts is a journey into the city's rich cultural heritage. Each handcrafted item tells a story, weaving together the threads of history, religion, and craftsmanship. Whether you are a visitor seeking a tangible memory of your time in Jerusalem or a local looking to celebrate and preserve the city's heritage, these souvenirs and traditional crafts offer a glimpse into the soul of this remarkable city, bridging the gap between past and present.

AUTHENTIC LOCAL MARKETS AND BAZAARS

Jerusalem is renowned for its vibrant and diverse markets and bazaars. These bustling marketplaces are not only a hub of economic activity but also offer visitors a fascinating glimpse into the city's rich history, traditions, and vibrant local culture. From the bustling streets of the Old City to the modern markets in the newer neighborhoods, Jerusalem's markets are a treasure trove of unique experiences and sensory delights.

The Old City Markets:

The Old City of Jerusalem is home to several iconic markets that have been thriving for centuries. Each of the four quarters—Muslim, Jewish, Christian, and Armenian—has its own distinct market area. The most famous among them is the Muslim Quarter's vibrant and bustling market, known as the "Souk."

Here, narrow winding alleyways are filled with stalls selling everything from spices and textiles to jewelry and traditional handicrafts. The aroma of spices wafts through the air, and the sounds of vendors haggling with customers create an atmosphere steeped in tradition and authenticity.

Mahane Yehuda Market:

Located in the western part of Jerusalem, Mahane Yehuda Market, also known as "The Shuk," is a lively and vibrant open-air market. Originally a place for locals to shop for fresh produce, it has transformed into a bustling market where you can find a wide variety of goods, including fruits, vegetables, spices, baked goods, cheeses, and more.

As you stroll through the market's narrow lanes, you'll encounter vendors showcasing their colorful wares and hear the lively banter between them and their customers.

The market also features trendy cafes, restaurants, and bars, making it a popular spot for locals and tourists alike.

Arab Shuk in East Jerusalem:

Located just outside the Old City's Damascus Gate, the Arab Shuk is a vibrant market that offers a unique experience. This bustling marketplace is predominantly frequented by Palestinians, and it provides a window into their culture, traditions, and culinary delights.

The market is a feast for the senses, with vendors selling fresh fruits, vegetables, meat, spices, sweets, and traditional Palestinian goods. It's an excellent place to sample delicious street food like falafel, hummus, and freshly squeezed juices while immersing yourself in the local ambiance.

Bezalel Arts and Crafts Fair:

For those interested in local art and crafts, the Bezalel Arts and Crafts Fair is a must-visit. Held on Fridays in the center of Jerusalem, near the Bezalel Academy of Arts and Design, this fair showcases the talents of local artisans.

From handmade jewelry and ceramics to paintings, sculptures, and textiles, you can find a wide range of unique and artistic creations. The fair provides an opportunity to meet the artists themselves, learn about their creative processes, and purchase one-of-a-kind souvenirs that reflect the essence of Jerusalem's artistic community.

Nachlaot Flea Market:

Located in the picturesque neighborhood of Nachlaot, this flea market is a hidden gem. Held on Fridays, it offers a charming and eclectic mix of vintage items, antiques, second-hand clothing, books, and various knick-knacks.

As you explore the market, you'll discover hidden treasures and engage in delightful conversations with the vendors, many of whom are passionate collectors and experts in their fields. Whether you're a collector, a vintage enthusiast, or simply looking for unique items, the Nachlaot Flea Market is a delightful place to spend a leisurely afternoon.

These are just a few examples of the authentic local markets and bazaars in Jerusalem. The city's markets are not only places to shop but also spaces where history, culture, and traditions intersect. They provide an immersive experience, allowing visitors to interact with locals, taste traditional foods, and discover unique handmade crafts.

Exploring these markets is a journey through time, reflecting the city's vibrant past and present, and offering a deeper understanding of Jerusalem's rich tapestry of cultures and traditions.

MODERN SHOPPING CENTERS AND MALLS:

Jerusalem, a city that resonates with historical and religious significance, has witnessed a transformation in its retail landscape with the advent of modern shopping centers and malls.

In recent years, these vibrant commercial spaces have become integral parts of the urban fabric, offering a diverse range of retail, entertainment, and dining options. This note explores the emergence of modern shopping centers and malls in Jerusalem, highlighting their impact on the city's economy, culture, and social life.

Economic Impact:

The establishment of modern shopping centers and malls in Jerusalem has had a significant economic impact on the city. These commercial spaces have attracted both local and international retailers, contributing to job creation and generating revenue. The presence of renowned brands and large-scale retail outlets has bolstered the city's appeal as a shopping destination, attracting tourists and visitors from near and far. This influx of visitors has resulted in increased spending and tourism-related revenues, boosting the local economy.

Retail Variety and Convenience:

Modern shopping centers and malls in Jerusalem have brought a remarkable variety of retail options under one roof.

From high-end fashion brands to electronics, home decor, and groceries, these commercial spaces cater to a wide range of consumer needs. Moreover, the convenience of having numerous stores in one location allows shoppers to compare prices, browse multiple options, and make informed purchasing decisions. The integration of modern amenities, such as ample parking, food courts, and entertainment facilities, adds to the overall shopping experience and enhances customer satisfaction.

Entertainment and Leisure:

Beyond retail therapy, modern shopping centers and malls in Jerusalem have become popular entertainment hubs. Many malls house multiplex cinemas, offering the latest movie releases and a comfortable viewing experience. Additionally, dedicated spaces for indoor games, arcades, and children's play areas provide entertainment for families. Some malls even host live events, concerts, and art exhibitions, contributing to the cultural vibrancy of the city.

Social Gathering Spaces:

Shopping centers and malls have evolved into social gathering spaces, acting as meeting points for friends and families. These venues offer an inclusive environment where people can meet, socialize, and spend quality time together. Cafés, restaurants, and food courts provide a diverse culinary experience, accommodating different tastes and dietary preferences. The ambiance and design of these malls often incorporate comfortable seating areas, encouraging visitors to relax and enjoy their surroundings.

Urban Development and Architecture:

The development of modern shopping centers and malls in Jerusalem has contributed to the city's urban growth and architectural evolution. Contemporary malls are often designed to seamlessly blend with the existing urban fabric, respecting the city's historical character while incorporating modern elements. Architects and designers pay close attention to aesthetics, creating visually appealing structures that enhance the overall cityscape. The presence of these well-designed commercial spaces has the potential to attract further investment and urban development in surrounding areas

The rise of modern shopping centers and malls in Jerusalem has brought numerous benefits to the city, both economically and socially. These commercial spaces have transformed the retail landscape, offering a diverse range of shopping options, entertainment, and leisure activities. They have become social hubs, providing spaces for gatherings, events, and cultural experiences.

Furthermore, the architectural integration of these malls within the cityscape contributes to Jerusalem's urban development. Overall, the emergence of modern shopping centers and malls in

Jerusalem reflects the city's ability to adapt and cater to the needs of its residents and visitors, while preserving its rich historical and cultural heritage.

CHAPTER NINE: ACCOMMODATION OPTIONS:

HOTELS IN DIFFERENT PRICE RANGES

Jerusalem, the vibrant and historic city, offers a diverse range of accommodation options for visitors from around the world. Whether you're seeking luxury, comfort, or budget-friendly options, there are hotels in Jerusalem that cater to every traveler's needs.

In this note, we will explore hotels in different price ranges to help you make an informed decision when planning your stay in Jerusalem.

Luxury Hotels:

The King David Hotel: Situated in the heart of Jerusalem, The King David Hotel is a landmark establishment known for its opulence and impeccable service. This iconic hotel offers luxurious rooms, elegant suites, and breathtaking views of the Old City. With its rich history and lavish amenities, The King David Hotel ensures a truly memorable stay.

Waldorf Astoria Jerusalem: Located near the Jaffa Gate, the Waldorf Astoria Jerusalem blends modern sophistication with timeless elegance. The hotel boasts spacious rooms, a spa, a rooftop pool, and fine dining options. Its convenient location provides easy access to major attractions, making it a top choice for discerning travelers.

Mid-Range Hotels:

Mamilla Hotel: Situated just steps away from the Old City walls, the Mamilla Hotel offers a stylish and contemporary ambiance. Its rooms and suites are designed with a mix of modern and traditional elements, and the rooftop terrace provides panoramic views of Jerusalem. With its central location and excellent amenities, the Mamilla Hotel offers a comfortable stay at a reasonable price.

Leonardo Plaza Hotel Jerusalem: Nestled in the heart of the city, the Leonardo Plaza Hotel Jerusalem provides comfortable rooms, a fitness center, and a seasonal outdoor pool. Its location near the lively Ben Yehuda Street ensures easy access to shopping, dining, and entertainment options. The hotel's affordability and convenient amenities make it a popular choice for many travelers.

Budget-Friendly Hotels:

Abraham Hostel Jerusalem: Offering a vibrant and social atmosphere, Abraham Hostel Jerusalem provides budget-friendly accommodation with a range of options, including dormitory-style rooms and private rooms. The hostel features a communal kitchen, a bar, and various common areas where guests can socialize and meet fellow travelers. Its central location makes it an ideal base for exploring the city on a budget.

The Post Hostel Jerusalem: Located in the lively downtown area, The Post Hostel Jerusalem offers affordable rooms, dormitories, and a variety of communal spaces. The hostel features a rooftop terrace, a bar, and organized activities, creating a fun and interactive environment for guests. Its affordability, friendly staff, and vibrant atmosphere make it a popular choice among budget-conscious travelers.

When it comes to accommodation in Jerusalem, there are hotels in various price ranges to suit different preferences and budgets. Luxury hotels like The King David Hotel and Waldorf Astoria Jerusalem offer a lavish experience, while mid-range options like Mamilla Hotel and Leonardo Plaza Hotel provide comfort and convenience. For those on a budget, Abraham Hostel Jerusalem and The Post Hostel Jerusalem offer affordable accommodation with a lively atmosphere. No matter which price range you choose, these hotels in Jerusalem strive to provide an enjoyable and memorable stay in this extraordinary city.

GUESTHOUSES AND HOTELS

Guesthouses and hostels in Jerusalem offer budget-friendly accommodation options for travelers from all over the world. These establishments cater to various needs, providing comfortable and affordable lodging in the heart of this historic city. Whether you're a solo traveler, a group of friends, or a family exploring Jerusalem, guesthouses and hostels provide a convenient and communal atmosphere to enhance your experience.

Affordable Accommodation: One of the primary advantages of guesthouses and hostels in Jerusalem is their affordability. These establishments are ideal for budget-conscious travelers who want to explore the city without breaking the bank. Compared to hotels, guesthouses and hostels offer significantly lower rates, making them an attractive option for backpackers and those looking to save money on accommodation.

Central Locations: Many guesthouses and hostels in Jerusalem are located in the heart of the city, providing easy access to major attractions, cultural sites, and religious landmarks. Whether you're interested in visiting the Western Wall, exploring the Old City, or experiencing the vibrant markets, staying in a guesthouse or hostel ensures that you're never too far away from the action.

Communal Atmosphere: Guesthouses and hostels are known for their communal atmosphere, fostering social interactions among travelers from diverse backgrounds. These establishments often have common areas such as shared kitchens, lounges, and dining spaces where guests can mingle, share travel experiences, and make new friends. The friendly and inclusive environment allows solo travelers to connect with like-minded individuals, creating lasting memories and potentially lifelong friendships.

Facilities and Services: Despite their affordable rates, guesthouses and hostels in Jerusalem offer a range of facilities and services to ensure a comfortable stay. Private or shared rooms are available, depending on your preference and budget. Shared bathrooms are common, although some establishments offer ensuite options. Additionally, many guesthouses and hostels provide amenities such as free Wi-Fi, laundry facilities, luggage storage, and communal spaces for relaxation or work.

Local Knowledge and Assistance: The staff at guesthouses and hostels in Jerusalem are often well-versed in the city's history, culture, and attractions. They can provide valuable insights, recommendations, and assistance in planning your itinerary. Whether you're seeking advice on the best local restaurants, hidden gems, or transportation options, the knowledgeable staff can offer valuable guidance to enhance your visit to Jerusalem.

Cultural Exchange: Staying in a guesthouse or hostel allows travelers to experience the local culture firsthand. These establishments often organize events, activities, or city tours that provide insights into Jerusalem's rich heritage, traditions, and customs. From organized walks through the Old City's narrow streets to cultural evenings featuring music and dance performances, guesthouses and hostels facilitate a deeper appreciation and understanding of Jerusalem's diverse cultural tapestry.

Flexibility and Convenience: Guesthouses and hostels typically offer flexible check-in and check-out times, accommodating travelers arriving at different hours. This flexibility is particularly beneficial for those with early or late flights or those who wish to maximize their time exploring the city. Additionally, many guesthouses and hostels offer additional services such as airport transfers, tour bookings, and assistance with arranging transportation, making it convenient for guests to navigate the city with ease.

In conclusion, guesthouses and hostels in Jerusalem offer an excellent accommodation option for travelers seeking affordability, central locations, and a communal atmosphere. These establishments provide not only a place to rest but also opportunities to connect with fellow travelers and immerse oneself in the rich cultural heritage of the city. Whether you're a solo adventurer or part of a group, staying in a guesthouse or hostel in Jerusalem can enhance your travel experience while staying within your budget.

VACATION RENTALS AND APARTMENTS

While hotels are a popular choice for accommodation, vacation rentals and apartments offer an alternative that allows visitors to delve deeper into the city's rich tapestry. In this note, we will explore the benefits and attractions of vacation rentals and apartments in Jerusalem, providing you with insights into the ideal options for your stay.

Authenticity and Cultural Immersion:
Choosing a vacation rental or apartment in Jerusalem provides an unparalleled opportunity to immerse yourself in the local culture. These accommodations are often situated in residential neighborhoods,

allowing you to experience daily life alongside the locals. From morning markets and bustling streets to local eateries and hidden gems, you can truly feel like a part of the community.

Flexibility and Comfort:

Vacation rentals and apartments offer a level of flexibility and comfort that is often unmatched by hotels. They provide ample space, including separate bedrooms, living areas, and fully equipped kitchens, enabling you to relax, unwind, and even prepare your meals at your own convenience. This flexibility is particularly advantageous for families, large groups, or travelers seeking a more private and intimate setting.

Cost-Effectiveness:

For budget-conscious travelers, vacation rentals and apartments in Jerusalem offer an excellent value proposition. These accommodations often have a more affordable price tag compared to hotels, especially when considering longer stays. Additionally, the option to cook your meals in the apartment's kitchen can help you save on dining expenses. With the money saved, you can allocate more resources to exploring the city's attractions, sampling local cuisine, or engaging in exciting activities.

Diverse Range of Options:

Jerusalem boasts a wide array of vacation rentals and apartments to cater to every taste and preference. Whether you're looking for a modern apartment in the heart of the city or a charming traditional home in a historic neighborhood, you'll find a plethora of choices. From luxury accommodations to cozy and quaint apartments, Jerusalem's rental market can accommodate various budgets, group sizes, and desired amenities.

Unique Locations and Neighborhoods:
Each neighborhood in Jerusalem possesses its distinct character and charm. From the ancient alleys of the Old City to the vibrant streets of downtown Jerusalem, you can find vacation rentals and apartments in diverse locations. You may opt for an apartment near the Western Wall, allowing you to explore the religious and historical sites with ease. Alternatively, you might choose a

rental in the trendy neighborhood of Mahane Yehuda, known for its lively market, culinary delights, and nightlife.

Professional Services and Support:

Vacation rental agencies and platforms in Jerusalem strive to provide visitors with top-notch service and support. Many offer reliable customer service, ensuring a smooth booking process and addressing any concerns or queries throughout your stay. Additionally, they often provide assistance in arranging transportation, tours, and local recommendations, allowing you to make the most of your time in the city.

When considering a visit to Jerusalem, vacation rentals and apartments present an attractive alternative to traditional hotel accommodation. Offering authenticity, cultural immersion, flexibility, cost-effectiveness, diverse options, unique locations, and professional services, these accommodations provide an exceptional way to experience the city. By choosing a vacation rental or apartment, you can create lasting memories while savoring the enchantment of Jerusalem from the comfort of a home away from home.

CHAPTER TEN

CLOSING NOTE:

Dear pilgrim, I urge you to create your own unique experience of Jerusalem, pay attention to every detail as you navigate the historic sites and enjoy all that Jerusalem has to offer. As I wish you a profound, breathtaking and fruitful pilgrim with lots of spiritual transformation in your life, I also pray for the success of your pilgrimage, Amen.

SUGGESTED ITINERARY FOR JERUSALEM PILGRIMS

Here's a suggested 6-day itinerary for a Jerusalem pilgrimage based on the proximity of the sites to each other:

Day 1: Old City Exploration

★Start your pilgrimage by exploring the Old City of Jerusalem, a UNESCO World Heritage site.

★Begin at the Western Wall, also known as the Wailing Wall, an important religious site for Jewish worshippers.

★Visit the Temple Mount, home to the Al-Aqsa Mosque and the Dome of the Rock.

★Explore the Christian Quarter, including the Church of the Holy Sepulchre, believed to be the site of Jesus' crucifixion, burial, and resurrection.

★Walk along the Via Dolorosa, the path Jesus is believed to have taken on the way to his crucifixion.

★End the day with a visit to the Jewish Quarter, where you can explore historical synagogues and the Cardo, a reconstructed ancient Roman street.

Day 2: Mount of Olives and Mount Zion

★Begin at the Mount of Olives, overlooking the Old City. Visit the Chapel of Ascension and the Church of All Nations in the Garden of Gethsemane.

★Walk down the Palm Sunday Road to the Church of Dominus Flevit and the Church of Mary Magdalene.

★Continue to Mount Zion and visit the Room of the Last Supper, believed to be the location of the Last Supper.

★Explore the nearby Church of St. Peter in Gallicantu, traditionally associated with Peter's denial of Jesus.

Day 3: Yad Vashem and Israel Museum

★Start the day with a visit to Yad Vashem, Israel's official memorial to the victims of the Holocaust. Explore the museum, the Hall of Remembrance, and the Children's Memorial.

★In the afternoon, head to the Israel Museum. See the famous Dead Sea Scrolls at the Shrine of the Book and explore the archaeological exhibits, including the Model of Ancient Jerusalem.

Day 4: Mount Herzl and Biblical Zoo

★Begin at Mount Herzl, Israel's national cemetery. Pay respects to prominent Israeli leaders and visit the Herzl Museum to learn about the visionary behind modern Zionism.

★In the afternoon, visit the Tisch Family Zoological Gardens, also known as the Biblical Zoo. Explore the zoo's diverse collection of animals with biblical references and enjoy the beautiful surroundings.

Day 5: Bethlehem Excursion

★Take a day trip to Bethlehem, located just outside Jerusalem. Visit the Church of the Nativity, believed to be the birthplace of Jesus.
★Explore the Milk Grotto, where tradition holds that Mary nursed baby Jesus.

★Visit the Shepherd's Field, a site associated with the shepherds who received news of Jesus' birth.

Day 6: Mount Scopus and Shrine of the Book

★Begin at Mount Scopus and enjoy panoramic views of Jerusalem. Visit the Hebrew University campus and the Hadassah Medical Center.

★Head to the Shrine of the Book, located in the Israel Museum, to see more Dead Sea Scrolls and learn about their significance.

Note: This itinerary provides a general outline and may require adjustments based on your specific interests, operating hours of the sites, and any religious observances or holidays that may affect access to certain locations. It is also best suited for personal use.

Printed in Great Britain
by Amazon

27666088R00183